A **BUSY** PERSON'S PILATES

SIMPLE ROUTINES FOR HOME, WORK AND TRAVEL

WRITTEN BY **ALAN HERDMAN** WITH **JO GODFREY WOOD**

This edition was published in the UK in 2003 exclusively for
WHSmith Limited, Greenbridge Road, Swindon SN3 3LD
www.WHSmith.co.uk
by Gaia Books Ltd., 66 Charlotte Street, London W1T 4QE
Copyright © 2003 Gaia Books Limited, London
Text copyright © 2003 Alan Herdman
Cover design © 2003 WHSmith Limited

ISBN 1 85675 1597

A catalogue record of this book is available from the British Library.

Printed and bound in China by Imago

10 9 8 7 6 5 4 3 2

A **BUSY** PERSON'S GUIDE TO
PILATES

Contents

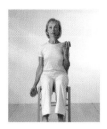

About Joseph Pilates

The Pilates exercise regime was devised by German-born Joseph Pilates (1880–1967). As a child he suffered from ill health and worked to overcome his frailty through gymnastics. By the time he was 14 his physique was so good that he found work as a model for anatomy charts. During World War I Pilates was interned in England, where he worked as a nurse to the other men, many of whom needed physical therapy. It was because of this that he started to develop equipment to help bed-ridden patients. By attaching springs to the walls over beds, patients could work on muscle strength, and it was noticed that they improved faster than the others.

After moving to Germany after the war, Pilates continued working on his fitness regime and met Rudolf von Laban, originator of the most widely used form of dance notation. Laban started to incorporate some of Pilates' exercises into his teaching. In 1926 Pilates moved to America and set up his first studio in New York, which became popular with dancers and attracted such legends as Martha Graham and George Balanchine. By the time Pilates died his method was still known only within the dance community, but has since found a far wider audience. As Pilates himself said, his innovations were "50 years ahead of my time".

ABOUT ALAN HERDMAN

Alan Herdman is a Laban-trained teacher of Dance Drama and he studied the Graham Technique at the London School of Contemporary Dance and the Pilates Technique in New York. He introduced Pilates to the UK in 1970 and has established exercise studios there and in several other countries. He teaches professional dancers, singers, actors, and all those who wish to improve their health. His first book, *Pilates, Creating the Body You Want*, is a worldwide best-seller.

Introduction

We all lead increasingly busy lives and while this can be stimulating, energizing, and fulfilling, sometimes we are left feeling overloaded, overstressed, and overtired. Life seems to be too much for us to cope with and we may feel worn out before the day has really begun. The physical activities we are asking the body to perform may be contributing to our general sense of unease and tension. For example, a high-pressure office job might require sitting for hours at the computer screen, or caring for a baby might mean constant heavy lifting and carrying.

While you can take rests from the computer or learn how to lift a heavy baby safely, Pilates can help you gain awareness of your body and help to strengthen it, too. With a strong body you can enjoy the physical challenges of your daily tasks. Yet the benefits of Pilates are not just physical: as your body becomes stronger and more supple, so too will your mind. You will find it easier to cope with everyday pressures, your concentration will improve, and you will be able to unwind easily at the end of the day. In short, regular Pilates will improve your quality of life.

THE HISTORY OF PILATES

The Pilates exercise regime encompasses a wide variety of exercises, some of which now vary significantly from the method originally devised by Joseph Pilates. A clear account of his original intentions are documented in his well-known classic book *Return to Life*. In this account, Pilates outlines his beliefs about modern living and the need for a harmoniously tuned life and body. He examines contemporary life, identifying the need for a well-balanced body, analyzing the effects of exercise on the blood and circulation, and suggesting healthy daily habits and routines to be acquired concerning diet, breathing, sleeping, and bathing. From these basic principles, Pilates created "Contrology" (later referred to simply as "Pilates"), describing his regime as the "complete coordination of the body, mind, and spirit".

Pilates taught that a balance of fresh air, sleep, a balanced diet, and exercise was vitally important for everyone and he perceived modern life to be counterproductive to achieving optimum health. He described the average adult as having a slumped body, stooped shoulders, hollow eyes, and flabby muscles, with lowered vitality. He felt that the trappings of modern civilization, such as telephones, cars, and economic pressures, were all contributing to widespread nervous tension and ill health and he developed Contrology in a bid to offset these effects.

Pilates designed his regime to encompass many elements, viewing the body on a neuro-muscular level, to unite mind and body, with Contrology enabling the person to exert control over muscles. He explored even muscle development, focusing on flexibility as well as strength. The result of practising Contrology would be to "stir your sluggish circulation into action and to perform its duty more effectively in the matter of discharging through the bloodstream the accumulation of fatigue-products created by muscular and mental activities. Your brain clears and your willpower functions" (Pilates, 1945). Pilates perceived his technique to be far more than a mere exercise system, describing Contrology to be a process of "gaining the mastery of your mind over the complete control of your body", resulting in improved self-esteem and confidence.

HOW TO USE THIS BOOK

Since Joseph Pilates first developed this system it has grown in popularity and is now one of the most widely practised mind–body exercise techniques ever, with a worldwide following. This book offers a complete range of simple Pilates techniques to fit in to your busy day, whether you travel to a workplace or spend your day at home. It covers the full range of physical activities you are likely to encounter, from the moment you wake up until you close your eyes at night. It is both a quick reference manual and a lifestyle guide. You can dip into it quickly or you can use it more systematically for an all-round healthy lifestyle, making the most of whatever physical activities you undertake. If you find that you have a few spare minutes, take the time to try out a new exercise. Make the most of these "stolen moments". As time goes by, you will gradually build an increased awareness of your body – your whole body, not just parts of it. You will start to have a "conversation" with your body as you develop your mind–body connection.

You may have already attended a Pilates studio for sessions comprising a mix of floor and apparatus exercises. If you have not, you can readily learn the techniques by following the instructions here. This book shows you how to incorporate Pilates into your life, no matter what you are doing, and without the need for equipment. You don't have to wear special clothes. You will soon find that you can easily relieve, for example, the strains caused by sitting or standing for too long, lifting heavy loads, or uncomfortable traveling conditions by doing some quick and easy Pilates exercises.

Chapter One, Introducing Pilates, explains how Pilates works. It then explains how to get started with Pilates, showing the workings of the main muscles and the importance of good posture. It also gives you basic Pilates theory and a section on warming up for all kinds of exercise plus general lifestyle advice. Chapter Two, Starting the day with Pilates, shows you how Pilates can get you off to a good start, while Chapter Three, Travelling with Pilates, will help you make any journey as comfortable and safe as possible, whether a short walk or a long plane journey. Chapter Four, Pilates at work, guides you through the working day, whether home- or office-based, while Chapter Five, Unwinding with Pilates, will help you leave a stressful day behind. Chapter Six, Pilates for pregnancy, gives exercises for making the months of pregnancy safer and more comfortable.

Alan Herdman

CHAPTER ONE

Introducing Pilates

Pilates is a gentle "thinking" exercise, helping your mind and body to work in harmony, to produce a healthy, toned, mobile body and a calm, relaxed mind. Using posture and breathing as key elements, Pilates is a non-aerobic exercise method, lengthening and strengthening the main muscles of the body.

Many kinds of sport and exercise regimes rely on the larger, more powerful, muscles to be effective and these become toned and strengthened as a consequence. We have often heard the phrase "no gain without pain" and we have become used to the idea that serious exercise must leave us feeling as though we have suffered, to some extent, before we can expect any benefits. As a result of this style of exercise (aerobic), the smaller muscles become under-used and weakened in comparison. However, in Pilates the smaller muscles are just as important as the larger ones and these, in time, become stronger, while the larger ones simply become more sleek and toned. Your muscle system, therefore, becomes perfectly in tune and a balanced, integrated whole.

In order to find these smaller muscle groups, you need firstly to learn how to locate them, and then you must learn how to use them. This needs a little determination and concentration and is why Pilates is often referred to as the "thinking" exercise. Because you do need to think, your mind and body have to work together and it is this effect that leads to a feeling of wholeness, calm, and inner peace, which will add greatly to the quality of your daily life and enable you to cope far better with its challenges.

This first chapter guides you through the muscles you need to know about for Pilates and how you can assess your posture before you start. It then outlines the vital eight principles of Pilates, how to warm up properly, and vital lifestyle information on food and sleep.

The effects of Pilates

The special kind of concentration that you have to pay to the smaller muscles is key to understanding and practising Pilates and is one of its eight main principles (see also pp.26–8). The other principles that you should be aware of are: centring, control, breathing, flowing movement, precision, individualization, and routine. It is important to take the time to understand these key concepts.

All the movements you make are small, gradual, and controlled and this makes them very safe for everyone to do, whether they are young or old, healthy, fit, or perhaps a little unfit.

While you are actually doing your Pilates exercises, you are gradually getting to know your own body, perhaps for the first time in your life. You find that as you learn and practise, you gradually start to experience results. At first, you may think that nothing much is happening and you are not aware of any changes. But soon you will feel that your posture is improving. Friends, family, or colleagues may unexpectedly tell you how well you look. Your muscles will start to feel more toned and your joints more flexible. Perhaps you notice that although you may not

necessarily lose weight, your stomach will become flatter and your limbs more toned and elongated in appearance. You will feel stronger and more in control of your body. Your overall sense of well-being will be evident to all who come into contact with you. And most importantly of all, you will feel calmer and more relaxed throughout the day, whatever activity you are undertaking.

IMPORTANT PILATES POINTS
- Get to know the 8 Pilates principles.
- Small movements are more important than big ones.
- Get to know your own body.
- Regular practice brings results.
- Your posture will soon improve.
- Your stomach will become flatter.
- You will soon start to feel good about yourself.

Your muscle groups

When you are doing Pilates exercises you are using your muscles in a very particular way. You are focusing them precisely and you are thinking about the quality of the movement. For example, you think about "how" you flex your leg rather than "how far". Many of your muscles will be used in synchronicity with each other. To begin with, you may think that your muscles are too weak to be able to do a particular exercise. You may not even

be able to find them at first. But if you persevere, gradually they will become more obvious and stronger. The pictures below show the main muscle groups you need to know about. If you are attending a Pilates studio, you will hear them mentioned by your instructor.

Trapezius
For raising and rotating the shoulder blades, and for lifting your arms above your head.

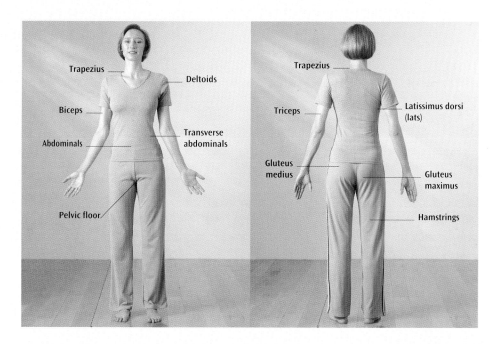

Trapezius — Deltoids
Biceps —
Abdominals — Transverse abdominals
Pelvic floor

Trapezius
Triceps — Latissimus dorsi (lats)
Gluteus medius — Gluteus maximus
Hamstrings

Deltoids
These are for moving the shoulders outward and backward and extending and flexing your arms.

Biceps
For bending the elbow and turning the forearm so that the palms are facing upward.

Abdominals
These are for flexing the abdomen, pulling your stomach toward your ribs and, when lying down, for lifting your shoulders and legs. The transverse abdominals hold your internal organs in place.

Lats
You use these muscles when doing pull-ups and when you breathe out they squeeze your ribs.

Gluts
These muscles are for extending the hip and rotating the thighs laterally. If you exercise them regularly, your buttock muscles will remain firm.

Triceps
For straightening or extending your forearm at the elbow.

Hamstrings
You use these muscles for flexing your knees and extending your thighs.

Pelvic floor
This is the thin diaphragm of muscles straddling the pelvic girdle. It is important for both women and men and should be kept in trim throughout life.

Obliques
For flexing and bending the trunk.

YOUR SKELETON
The skeleton is the basic framework of the body, giving it its fundamental form. While the eventual sizes and proportions of individual bones are determined long before birth, the way they are balanced can change and shift throughout life. This depends on how you hold yourself, how you move, what postural habits you adopt, and your overall health and well-being.

Assess your posture

Did you assume that you had good posture until you caught sight of your reflection in a shop window? Were you shocked at how bad your posture looked? Did you look slightly stooped or did your clothes look ill-fitting? One of the key elements of Pilates is posture. The exercises make you think about it and improve it and one of Pilates' great benefits is the graceful posture that you eventually achieve. Good posture, apart from making you look and feel good and contributing to your overall good health and well-being, helps you get maximum benefits out of Pilates. For example, holding in your abdominal muscles will stop you straining your back during Pilates exercises. Equally, in everyday life, good posture will help prevent back pain – responsible for more lost working days than any other ailments.

In short, Pilates helps you improve your posture, and good posture, in turn, helps you get the most out of Pilates.

GOOD OR BAD POSTURE?

Before you start to assess your posture, think about the following important points:

- Does your chin jut out or point upward? If so, your spine is out of alignment, shortening the muscles at the back of your neck.
- Are your shoulders the same height or is one higher than the other?
- When your arms hang down loosely by your sides, are your wrists the same distance from your hips as each other?
- Are your knees straight, pointing to the front?
- Are both of your feet flat on the ground?
- Is your weight distributed toward the outside or inside edges of your feet, or toward the back or the front?

The pictures on the following pages (pp.16–24) show you how you can assess and improve your posture. Use page 25 to determine which Pilates exercises would be best for you to improve your posture.

FRONT VIEW/INCORRECT
The weight of the body is being carried on one side, causing the shoulders to be lop-sided and the hips unevenly balanced. The spine is out of alignment and curved to one side. The knees point inward and the feet are pigeon-toed. The result is that the clothes pull uncomfortably in different directions and hang unevenly.

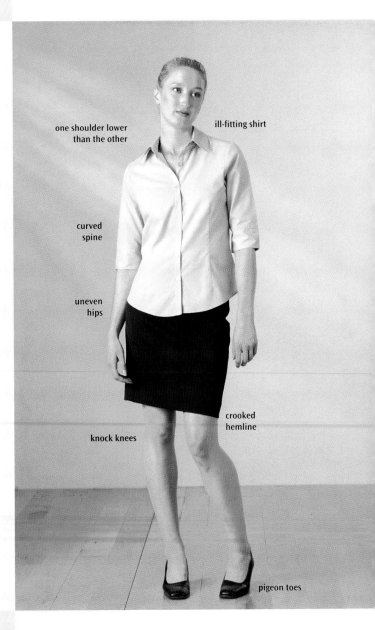

one shoulder lower than the other

ill-fitting shirt

curved spine

uneven hips

crooked hemline

knock knees

pigeon toes

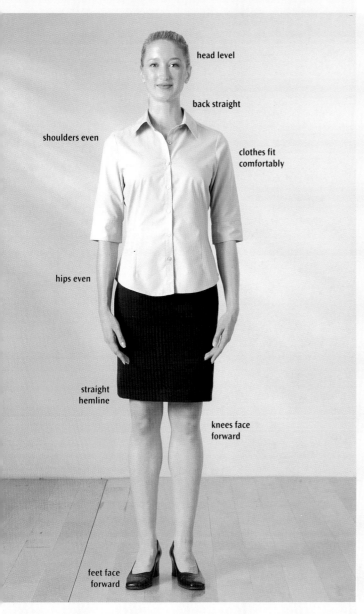

head level

back straight

shoulders even

clothes fit
comfortably

hips even

straight
hemline

knees face
forward

feet face
forward

FRONT VIEW/CORRECT

Adopting correct posture will allow your clothes to hang evenly, fit comfortably, and your hemline will be straight. To correct your head position, look ahead, with your chin pulled gently back. Imagine a piece of string attached to the top of your head pulling upward, making your neck and spine longer. You may well be storing tension in your neck. Look and see whether your shoulders and upper back roll forward. Are your shoulders at even heights? If you tend to carry a bag on one shoulder, you may be in the habit of tensing one side and not the other. Let your shoulders drop and if they get tense, loosen them up by rotating them a few times.

SIDE VIEW/INCORRECT

Stand sideways on to the mirror. Does your lower back curve in, or your stomach or bottom stick out? Do you tend to support your body weight mainly on one side? In this example the girl is supporting her weight mainly on the left side, so that the pelvis and spine are lop-sided. The shoulders are hunched and uneven. The bottom protrudes and the back is curved inward.

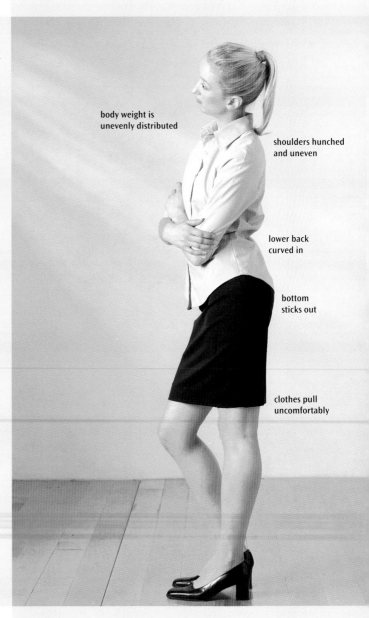

body weight is
unevenly distributed

shoulders hunched
and uneven

lower back
curved in

bottom
sticks out

clothes pull
uncomfortably

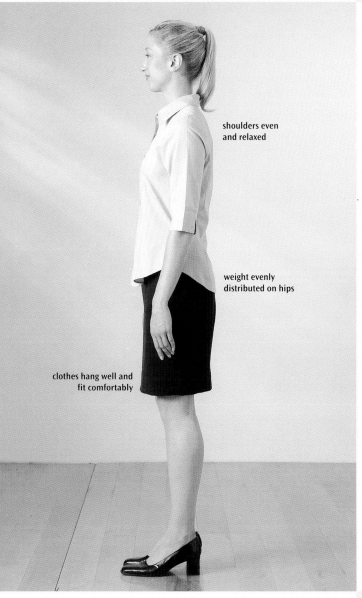

shoulders even
and relaxed

weight evenly
distributed on hips

clothes hang well and
fit comfortably

SIDE VIEW/CORRECT

Your legs should be straight and the resulting stretched feeling should extend all the way up to the buttock muscles. Try drawing your stomach in. This will make your pelvis tilt. Hold this position by squeezing the lowest muscles in the buttocks. Your choice of shoes is important. Avoid very high heels and platforms and choose soles which are flexible, allowing the foot maximum movement.

THE ROLL DOWN

To check that there is no tension in your neck and shoulders and that you are using the correct muscles.

■ *Stand with feet apart, knees bent, and fingers easy. Squeeze your butt and hold your stomach in.*

■ *Drop chin to chest, feeling the stretch down to your upper back. Let your shoulders and upper back roll forward.*

■ *Let your arms drop in front and your back curve more. Keeping your legs bent, let your upper body hang upside down, your head stretching your spine.*

■ *Keeping your knees bent and arms hanging, slowly come upright. First gently squeeze your butt and pull your stomach in. Unroll your spine, concentrating on the front of your body. Feel your shoulders slide downward, keeping your arms loose. Slowly straighten your knees and feel your neck lengthen, placing your head slightly forward.*

01

02

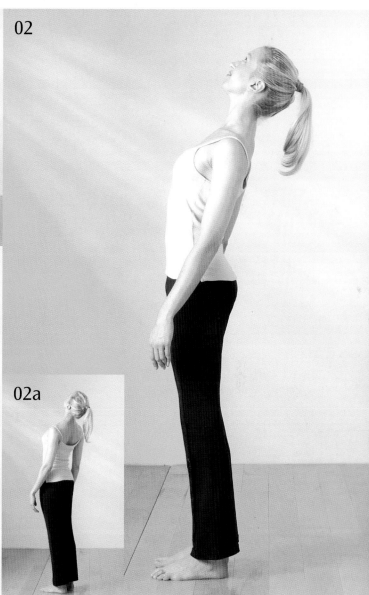

LEANING BACK *(01–02)*
*To assess the mobility of
your upper back.*

*(01) Stand straight, arms
hanging loosely.*

*(02) From your thoracic
spine, lift up through your
torso and direct your
sternum toward the ceiling.
Let your arms hang
naturally. Don't be tempted
to force your body backward
– you will overbalance.*

02a

*(02a) The same posture as
Step (02), giving more details
of the back view.*

01

02   03

TWIST/COSSACK *(01–03)*
To check the mobility of your thoracic spine.

(01) Hold your hands flat in front of you, with your fingertips butting together, in the middle of your sternum.

(02) Breathe in, and as you breathe out, turn your upper body to the right. Breathe in again and return to the centre.

(03) Breathe in, and as you breathe out, turn your upper body to your left side. Breathe in again and return to the centre. Repeat the cycle 10 times.

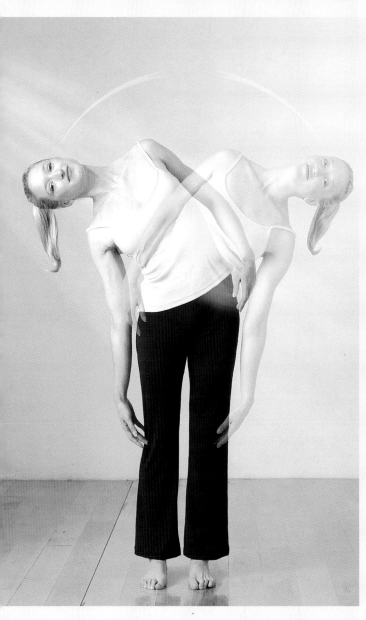

SIDE-BENDING

To check your overall mobility and see whether your side-stretch is equal on both sides of your body.

Stand normally and let your hands hang softly and naturally. Breathe in, and as you breathe out, bend over on one side, thinking of your ear going over toward your shoulder. Breathe in again, and as you breathe out, come up to your starting position again. Repeat the bend on the other side of your body and repeat the cycle 10 times.

01   **02**

HAMSTRINGS (01–02)
To check the mobility of your hamstrings.

(01) Lie on the floor with your right knee bent and your foot flat on the floor. Point your left foot upward, with long toes and a slight flex. Don't let your toes curl. Draw your stomach muscles down toward the floor.

(02) Breathe in, and as you breathe out, raise your left leg to the vertical position. Breathe in, and as you breathe out, lower the leg again. Repeat for your right leg. Repeat the cycle 10 times.

HOW DID YOU DO?

You may have noticed that some aspects of your posture need working on. When you have identified any of the common problems listed below, work carefully through Chapters Two, Three, Four, and Five to help remedy them. You can select a quick, personal routine to use on a regular basis. The main areas to concentrate on are: abdominals, buttocks, hamstrings, inner thighs, and lats.

Q *When you stand sideways-on to the mirror does your:*
■ *stomach stick out?* ■ *bottom stick out?* ■ *lower back curve inward?*

A *If so you need to tone your abdominals, buttock muscles, hamstrings, and lats.*

Q *Are your shoulders tense and stiff or rounded?*

A *If so you need shoulder and lats exercises and exercises affecting the middle of your back.*

Q *Does your behind sag and do your knees look bent?*

A *Strengthen your centre, paying particular attention to your buttocks. Strengthen your hamstrings and then stretch them.*

Q *Do you find it hard to stand up straight? Does your body feel uncomfortable?*

A *You need to tone all your muscle groups to attain good posture and a feeling of well-being.*

The key principles of Pilates

The aim of the Pilates method is to turn your mind and body into a single entity, so that you can move effortlessly, gracefully, and safely, without having to think twice about it. But before this can happen, you have to train your mind to think about your body while you are doing the exercises. You have to pay your body your full attention. To do this, there are eight basic principles that you should try to carry out whenever you are doing Pilates exercises.

1. CONCENTRATION

With many exercise techniques, you can mentally "switch off" when you are doing the physical exercises. But with Pilates, every tiny movement requires you to think carefully. This means that you must block out other thoughts while you concentrate. When you are doing the Pilates exercises, follow the directions exactly and do not be tempted to take short cuts. Bring your whole attention to what you are doing. Operate in the present and practise mindfulness. Do not assume that you already know how to do something when you could well benefit from running through the instructions again. Concentrate fully on what you are doing

and on your entire body. This is important because movements that you might assume are simple may actually be more complex than you think. In Pilates, every position and movement of every part of the body is interrelated. Each affects and has impact on the other. To concentrate on your whole body, all at once, is a particular challenge, but it will come with practice. Once you have it, it will help you in both work and leisure, as a fusion of mind and body.

2. CENTRING

"Centring" as a term used in Pilates has nothing to do with the Eastern "spiritual centre" or "centring down", which you may have heard of. One of the basic aims of Pilates is to strengthen the deep, core muscles. The idea is to protect the spine and create a strong base for you to carry out ordinary movements. Centring is vital for your every movement, whether you are running a race or just sitting quietly in a chair. Your centre is the continuous band of muscles stretching between the bottom of your ribcage and across your hipbones. This is your focal point. If you keep it supple, your waist will remain trim, your stomach will be flat, your posture will be improved, and you will experience less tiredness, less niggling back pain, and fewer injuries in general. Your centre represents your core stability.

3. CONTROL
Pilates exercises are not random activities. Concentration on your body helps you to control every aspect of every movement you make, from the minute positioning of your fingertips to expansive limb movements. If you make wild, uncontrolled movements without really thinking about what you are doing, this will be echoed in the other physical activities you carry out in your life. It therefore follows that controlled physical activities will allow you to be more controlled about your thoughts and behaviour. You will be in charge of your self rather than letting it be in charge of you. Because you are working against gravity in Pilates, your body is gradually strengthened. The more slowly you are make movements, through heightened control, the greater will be your strength and your co-ordination. You will achieve greater benefits from Pilates.

4. BREATHING
Breathing is one of the key focuses of Pilates. Proper breathing means that the blood can be charged with oxygen and can do its work efficiently, awakening all the body's cells and carrying away wastes. When you are doing Pilates exercises, your breathing must be properly co-ordinated with the movement you are making, so it is important to make sure that you follow all the breathing instructions given in the exercises exactly. As a general rule, breathe in to prepare (or to return to the centre/starting place during an exercise) and breathe out to carry out the movement. There are exceptions to this instruction, and they are clearly stated where they apply.

5. FLOWING MOVEMENT
Pilates exercises should be carried out smoothly and evenly in order to receive the maximum benefit possible. Try not to move too stiffly or jerkily, nor too quickly, nor too slowly. When you walk down the street, one muscle should work in conjunction with another. There should be a synchronicity of your movements with each other.

6. PRECISION

If you carry out all the little movements as exactly as you can, they will have more impact and more lasting value. You will start to experience your body as being finely tuned, and this state is then echoed in your everyday life as grace and economy of movement.

7. INDIVIDUALIZATION

Each of us is different and each of us has our different needs and abilities. Learning how to do Pilates lets us build up an awareness of our own body, which will eventually develop control of individual muscle groups and correct movement patterns.

8. ROUTINE

Pilates requires regular practice in order to have any impact on your body and then on your lifestyle. The technique does not replace other activities but is a way of enhancing your own performance in them and in life in general. So make Pilates a regular habit in your everyday life, whatever you are doing. This book lets you know how to integrate Pilates in your everyday life, even when you are away from home on a business trip or on holiday.

WARMING UP

If you are about to start on a demanding physical activity, warm up properly beforehand, working the cardiovascular and respiratory systems together. Here are some ideas on which to build your own warm-up routine:

■ Start by walking around, changing directions continually. Your feet should remain soft and your joints relaxed. Build up speed. Start rotating your shoulders forward and backward. Rotate your wrists and move your fingers. Circle your arms in both directions, with bent elbows and then straight. Now turn your torso in the direction of the circle. Gradually increase your pace until you break into a gentle run. Keep your feet soft and your joints relaxed. Continue to move your arms, piston fashion. Decrease speed until you return to walking pace.

■ Stand with feet slightly apart, knees straight but not locked. Place your fingers on your shoulders with your elbows out to the sides and your upper arms parallel to the floor. Circle your elbows backward and forward, feeling the movement in the shoulder joints.

■ Place your arms by your sides, palms facing backward. As you breathe out, without moving your shoulders, slowly press your arms backward. This movement works on your lats.

■ Now fold your arms in front of your chest, away from your breast bone. Keeping your hips very still, breathe in, and as you breathe out, turn your torso as far to your right as possible, and breathe in as you return to the centre. Repeat on the other side.

■ Place your feet further apart. Put your left hand on your hip, elbow out to the side, and stretch your right arm upward. As you breathe out, keeping your hips still, stretch your torso to your left, holding the stretch. Increase the stretch by rotating your palm upward. Repeat on the other side.

■ Return to your basic standing position. Drop your head to your chest and as you breathe out, roll your spine down as far as you can, allowing your arms to hang. Breathe in, and as you breathe out, slowly roll back up to the starting position. Repeat 10 times.

■ Now gently stretch your calves, hamstrings, and quads. Go slowly into the stretch and hold for ten to fifteen seconds. Do not bounce.

■ Turn your attention to your hands and feet. Resting with one foot off the ground, supported, move your ankle joint through its full range. Using your hands, manipulate the toe joints and then stretch and massage them.

■ After activity, it is important to cool down. It is necessary to slowly reduce your body temperature to a normal level. Gradually reduce your pace of movement and stretch your major muscles.

WARM-UP SUMMARY
1. *Walk around and loosen up*
2. *Stand and circle your shoulders*
3. *Work on your lats*
4. *Torso rotation*
5. *Torso stretching*
6. *Head on to chest*
7. *Stretch calves, hamstrings, and quads*
8. *Hands and feet*
9. *Cool down*

Your busy lifestyle

It doesn't matter how much exercise you do, or how sensible you are about your posture, if you are existing on a poor diet of convenience foods, indulging in too much alcohol, smoking, and not getting enough sleep, your general health will start to suffer. Taking extra exercise will not help. You will feel constantly tired and on edge, low in energy, and have difficulty concentrating. Your work will begin to suffer and your social life will, too. You will start succumbing to minor illnesses such as colds and flu and you may even start to feel depressed. You need to take stock of your life and how you live it. Then, having made a few basic adjustments, you will start to feel and look better, and be able to cope with all the demands made of you during the course of your day.

FOOD CHOICES

A balanced diet is crucial for your good health, so it is well worth spending a little time and energy planning your daily food intake. Rather than just grabbing a bite to eat whenever you feel hungry, try to plan to eat three regular, nutritious meals a day and think carefully about your snacks, too.

Many people indulge in a little snack, such as a chocolate bar or a packet of crisps, when they're feeling bored or stressed, and not necessarily because they are feeling genuinely peckish. This may spoil their appetite for the next meal as they take on board "empty" calories and don't have room for a proper meal. It is very tempting to get a quick "sugar-fix" from something sweet, which will give you instant energy, but will leave you feeling drained and lethargic later on. Try to resist this temptation. If you do have snacks, choose a piece of fruit such as a banana, a handful of unsalted nuts, or a crunchy carrot instead of fatty convenience snacks.

If you are trying to lose weight, bear in mind that eating less will not necessarily do the trick on its own, particularly if yours is a sedentary lifestyle. You need to combine a healthy food intake that is right for your own needs with increased exercise.

Most of us have only a vague awareness of what a good, balanced diet should consist of. We may be aware that we should hold back on the red meat and fatty foods and eat more fresh fruit, vegetables, and fibre, yet it is hard to know whether we are really getting a good balance of nutrients. In general, it is the quality of what you consume that matters rather than the quantity, because individual needs vary dramatically according to height, age, frame, metabolism, and levels of activity. However, a rule of thumb is to avoid eating a helping that is more than the equivalent of what would fill your own cupped hands. And try to shop for whole, unrefined foods that do not contain additives – if possible try to buy organically grown foods. It is important to drink plenty every day, too. You should aim to drink at least two litres (3.5 pints) a day of pure, filtered water to keep your body properly hydrated. It is particularly important to drink copiously when you are taking a plane journey (see p.63). Try to cut down on coffee, tea, and any other drinks containing caffeine, including some cola-type drinks, as they have a dehydrating effect.

You should aim to eat a diet that contains a balance of acid- and alkaline-based foods. Acid-forming foods include meat, eggs, fish, game, starches, and flour products. Alkaline foods include all fruits, plus green and root vegetables. A guideline is to have a ratio of one to four (one part acid to four parts alkaline). For example, if you have one portion of cheese, fish, meat, or bread, you should accompany it with four parts of fruit, and green or root vegetables.

It is a good idea to try to eat five portions of fresh fruit and vegetables per day and up to four slices of wholemeal bread. If you are a meat-eater, eat fish once or twice per week, poultry once or twice, and red meat only once. Be sparing with cheese and have pastry only occasionally. Restrict your alcohol intake to one or two glasses of wine with your evening meal and try not to make a habit of drinking alcohol every night. Try, also, to watch your intake of refined sugars – often hidden in low-fat convenience foods, ready-made meals, sweets and biscuits – and refined carbohydrates (for example, bread, pasta, and white rice). These can upset the blood sugar levels and encourage mood swings, energy dips, hyperactivity, and weight gain. Instead, choose complex carbohydrates, which release sugar into the blood stream more slowly, such as whole grains, beans, lentils, and vegetables.

FOOD GROUPS
Carbohydrates and fibre
Present in: grains, fruits, pulses, nuts, vegetables, and milk. Starch-rich foods such as whole grains, root vegetables, pulses, and bananas should make up half your calorie intake.

Fats
Made up of saturated, polyunsaturated, and monounsaturated fatty acids. Consuming a mixture of foods gives a balanced diet. Be aware that animal fats and margarines contain more saturated fatty acids than vegetable fats.

Proteins
Found in all fruits and vegetables, especially peas, beans, lentils, grains, nuts, seeds, sprouted seeds, and potatoes. Animal proteins are milk, cheese, meat, eggs, and fish.

Minerals
A variety of foods will give you the minerals you need.

Vitamins
Found in a variety of foods.

General tips
- Try to have lots of fibre – in pulses, whole grains, fruit, and vegetables.
- Have a generous selection of fresh fruit and vegetables, particularly green leafy ones, for your quota of vitamins, minerals, essential fatty acids, and fibre. Cook lightly or eat raw.
- Reduce your fat intake. Eat plenty of fish, offal, game, poultry, whole grains, pulses, nuts, and seeds and try to reduce red meat and cheese.
- Avoid cakes, sweets, chocolate, puddings, ice cream, jam, fruits canned in syrup, soft drinks, sugar in tea and coffee, and milk shakes.
- Cut down on processed foods to avoid saturated fats, added sugar, and refined grains and additives.
- Drink alcohol moderately.
- To lose weight, exercise more and eat a balanced diet. Do not eat more than you need to allow you to keep to the right weight for your height, age, and frame.

SLEEP

We all need good-quality sleep and plenty of it (usually about seven or eight hours a night), though it is common to hear of high-flying individuals who claim to survive on far less than the rest of us. We need sleep to be able to function well in life and losing even a little sleep affects our ability to function at our best levels. Chronic lack of sleep can stop children growing, reduce our immunity levels, and it can affect our ability to concentrate and make decisions.

A large number of issues can influence our ability to get the right amount of good-quality sleep. These can range from minor worries about work, relationships, finances, and health, through to persistent anxieties and depression. If you are having trouble getting to sleep, see whether you can reduce any of your worries first, then take a hard look at your lifestyle (see right).

Sleep tips

- Are you getting enough exercise? Aim to take about 15 minutes' brisk walk a day.
- Are you drinking too much caffeine? Choose dandelion coffee and herbal teas instead.
- Try not to eat a heavy meal later than 8pm.
- Is your bed right for you? It should be firm, but allow your spine to take up its natural S-shape.
- Are you too hot? Make sure your bed coverings are light but warm.
- Try a few drops of lavender or chamomile essential oil on your pillow.
- Are you getting enough fresh air in your bedroom? Keep a small window open, but do not sleep in a draught.
- Is artificial light shining into your bedroom? Invest in thick curtains or blinds to make your room as dark as possible.

CHAPTER TWO

Starting the day with Pilates

How you begin the day is important. Have you ever come out with, "I must have got out of bed on the wrong side today"? A shaky start can upset you, setting off a chain reaction turning into the classic "bad day". Pilates exercises can get you off to the best possible start to your day, helping you to achieve your true potential.

Before you even set foot out of bed it is a good idea to do some flexing Pilates exercises to get you going. Following these is a complete Pilates Bedroom Routine, to be done when you have just got out of bed, which will help you stretch and flex parts of the body that have been inactive overnight. In the bathroom section there are Pilates exercises that you can incorporate into your morning routine and there is useful advice about the right posture to adopt when you are brushing your teeth, and washing and brushing your hair.

Some people have problems balancing on one foot while they put on socks, tights, or trousers, and this is particularly hard to do in the mornings. Here we offer some simple Pilates exercises to gradually improve your all-round balance and flexibility and also make it easier to reach back fastenings.

At the breakfast table and in the kitchen, there are straightforward Pilates exercises you can do to relax and compose yourself for the coming day and easy ways you can carry out essential daily chores without damaging your posture.

Many people have to catch an early train, or they have children to attend to at this time in the morning, so exercising is low on their list of priorities. If this sounds like you, you may not have the time to do Pilates at this point in the day. Don't worry. Choose a quiet moment later on, when you are less rushed and can spend a few minutes on yourself.

In the bedroom

When you first wake up, make sure that your day starts well by thinking about the physical movements involved in getting out of bed. Perhaps it might be a good idea to wake a little earlier than usual, so that you have enough time to do some Pilates exercises in a relaxed frame of mind. Most people are woken by an alarm clock and leap out of bed far too suddenly. This violent reaction is bad for both body and soul and your day will get off to a bad start as a result.

Make a more leisurely start and take your time with a few gentle exercises in bed, which will help you compose yourself and your body for the day ahead. Try not to rush. After that, take a few minutes to do some gentle floor exercises, followed by a few more that you can combine with your morning bathroom routine. Then take your time selecting clothes and getting ready. Try to relish and enjoy each step of your preparation for the day ahead.

GENERAL TIPS
■ *When you purchase a mattress choose one that is neither too hard nor too soft, but firm and supportive. There should be some "give" in it, but not so much that your pelvis is pulled out of alignment.*
■ *Your pillow(s) should be feather-filled if possible and be reasonably flat, so that you are not sleeping with your head raised.*

THE FOETAL POSITION
If you have back problems of any sort, or even a somewhat "delicate" back, sleep in the cosy foetal position (see left), placing a flat pillow between your thighs and another under your head.

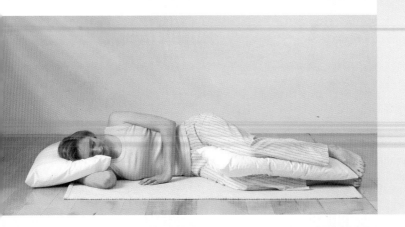

01

02

03

KNEE TO CHEST *(01–03)*
Do this exercise before you get out of bed, to help release any tension stored in your back and neck. You may not have even noticed that you are holding on to tension, but you will become aware of your posture improving once you have freed up your back and neck. You will feel your lower vertebrae opening up as you do the exercise.

(01) Lie on your back and bend your knees, keeping them in line with your hips, and slightly apart. Draw your stomach muscles in and hold until you have completed the exercise. Clasp your hands below your knees.

(02) Breathe in, and as you breathe out, gently pull your right knee down to your chest. Keep your arms away from your body. Breathe in again, and as you breathe out, pull your left knee down to your chest.

(03) Breathe in, and as you breathe out, pull both knees to your chest. Release. Repeat the cycle 10 times.

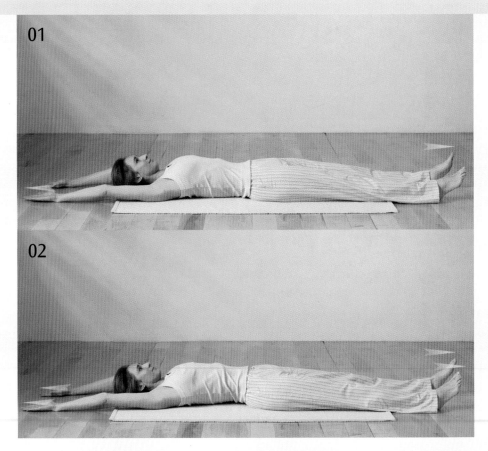

ARMS AND LEGS STRETCH (01–02)

This refreshing exercise stretches your body out fully. It is particularly effective if you have been sleeping in a curled-up position all night. You can do it either while you are still in bed or on the floor.

(01) Lying on your back, with arms and legs extended, breathe in. As you breathe out, stretch your right arm above your head as far as you can, and your left leg downward as far as possible. Then switch to your left arm and your right leg and do the same. Do this alternating sequence 8 times.

(02) Breathe in again. Then, as you breathe out, stretch both arms and legs simultaneously.

01

02

03

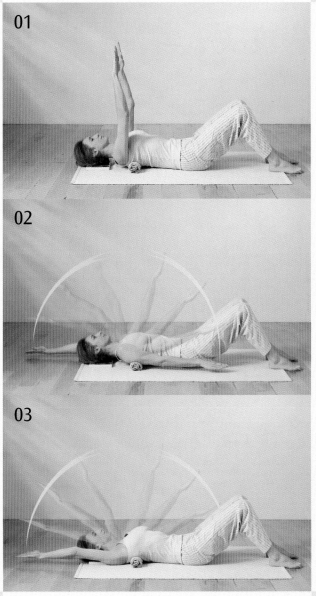

PILATES BEDROOM ROUTINE *(01–12)*
Try this simple Pilates floor sequence.

UPPER BACK RELEASE *(01–03)*
To release the shoulders and mobilize the thoracic spine.

(01) Lie on your back with knees up and feet flat. Put a small rolled hand towel under your shoulder blades and, if it feels comfortable, raise your head slightly with a paperback book. Stretch your arms softly upward, with fingers straight and palms facing forward.

(02) Breathe in, and as you breathe out again, draw your stomach muscles in, taking your left arm back by your ear. At the same time, move your right arm forward, against your side, fingers toward your toes.

(03) Breathe in as you take your arms back to the starting position and as you breathe out, take your right arm back and move your left arm forward. Carry on alternating your arms, about 10 times.

04

05

HIP ROLLS (04–05)

To stretch the waist and thighs, working the hips and lower back. Take great care if you have a lower back problem.

(04) Still lying on your back, with knees raised and feet flat on the floor, place your arms under your head. Your knees should be shoulder-width apart throughout.

(05) Take a breath in, and as you breathe out, move your knees across toward the floor on your right side. Your left buttock will lift off the floor slightly. As you do this, turn your head toward your left side. Breathe in, and as you breathe out, return your knees and head to the centre. Now repeat the movement for your other side. Alternate 10 times.

BUT SQUEEZE *(06–7)*

To strengthen the gluts, lengthen the lumbar spine, and activate the abs, so helping posture.

(06) Turn on to your front and place a small cushion between your thighs. Support your stomach with a pillow. Rest your head on your hands or to one side.

(07) Take a breath in. As you breathe out, focus on the cushion between your thighs by squeezing your buttock muscles, as if your "sitting bones" were pulling together. Try not to move your legs as this will over-use the buttock and leg muscles.

REST POSITION

Take a moment to rest completely. This position is perfect for releasing stresses and strains.

(08) Draw back from your face-down position (remove the cushions), so that your buttocks rest on your heels, your arms out in front. You will feel your back stretching along its length. Rest for a couple of minutes.

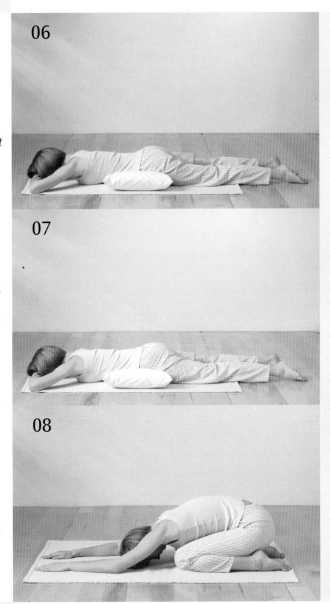

06

07

08

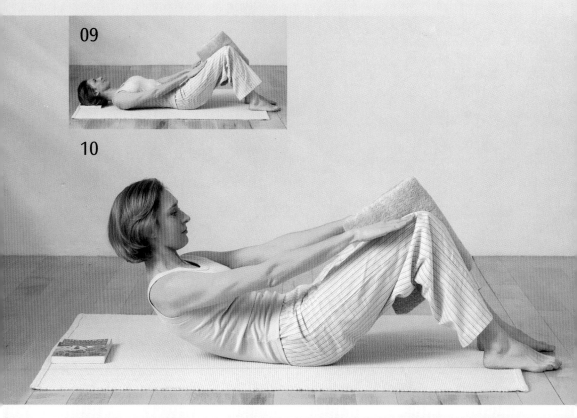

SIT-UPS (09–10)
To strengthen the abdominal muscles. You can do these in bed or on the floor.

(09) Lie on your back with knees raised and support your head with a folded towel or paperback book. Put a small towel between your knees and place your hands on your thighs so that your pelvis remains stable.

(10) Breathe in, and as you breathe out, draw your stomach muscles in and gently squeeze your inner thighs together, making sure your tailbone remains on the floor. Walk your fingers up your thighs, allowing your head and shoulders to curl gently off the floor. Breathe in, and as you breathe out, draw your stomach muscles in and roll back down, sliding your fingers down your legs again. Take a deep breath and rest. Do this sequence 10 times.

11

12

OBLIQUE SIT-UPS (11–12)
To work on the abdominal muscles at the sides of the body.

(11) Lie on your back in the same way as before, but with your left hand behind your head and your right hand flat by your side. Breathe in, and as you breathe out, draw your stomach muscles in.

(12) Supporting your head with your left hand, curve across your body, pointing your left elbow toward your right knee. Direct your gaze toward your right side, too. Stretch your right hand toward your feet. Breathe in, and as you breathe out, ease back to your starting position. Do 10 sit-ups on each side.

In the bathroom & kitchen

Make use of the moments you spend in the bathroom and kitchen to improve your posture and learn how to complete everyday tasks without putting unnecessary strain on your body.

GENERAL SELF-HELP

- Do not rush through your morning routine. Carry out your tasks mindfully, concentrating on what you are doing now rather than on what you will be doing later.
- Work on your posture to help you feel more confident about the busy day ahead.
- Take the time to eat a proper breakfast.

AT THE BASIN *(01–02)*
A standing cat exercise.

(01) Place your hands on either side of the basin, feet parallel. With your head bending softly, breathe in, and as you breathe out, let your back gently curve over.

(02) Breathe in. As you breathe out, lengthen your spine and pull your shoulders down. Arch your lower back and bring your head up. Breathe in and relax your back. Breathe out and elongate your spine again. Repeat 8–10 times.

UPPER BODY RELEASE
(03–04)
To work on your upper body posture. Shoulders are soft and easy.

(03) With your upper arms close to your body, bend your elbows to a 90-degree angle.

(04) Breathe in, and as you breathe out, trace a semicircle on either side. Make sure your upper arms remain close to your body. As you breathe in, return to your starting position. Repeat 10 times.

01 02

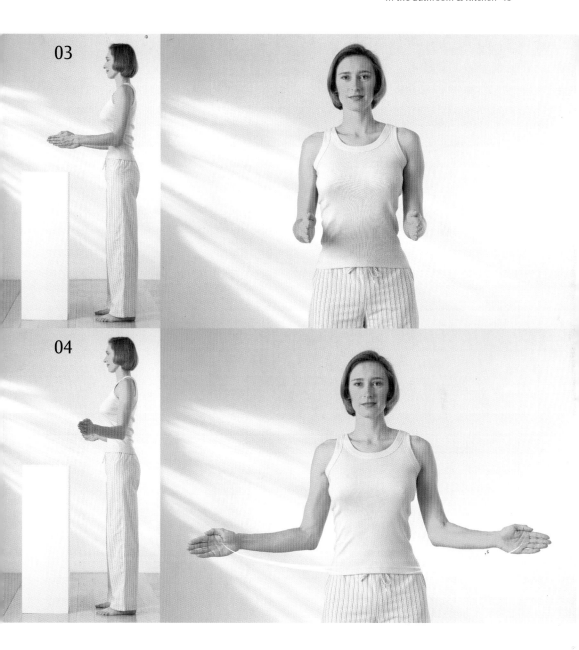

03

04

TEETH-BRUSHING

(01) The wrong way. Don't bend over with shoulders hunched, as shown here.

(02) Keep your back straight, and position one leg in front of the other. Lean forward from your waist.

HAIR-WASHING

If you have a delicate back and cannot bend over a hand basin, use a walk-in shower or kneel over the bath and use a hand attachment. Place a towel within easy reach.

(03) If your back is strong, keep your knees slightly bent as you incline your upper body and draw your abdominals in. Shampoo and rinse your hair thoroughly. Squeeze it out by hand. Reach for your towel and wrap it around your hair while you are still bent over. As you straighten up again, keep your knees bent and straighten them only after you have come upright. If you have one hand free and need some extra balance, hold the hand basin on one side.

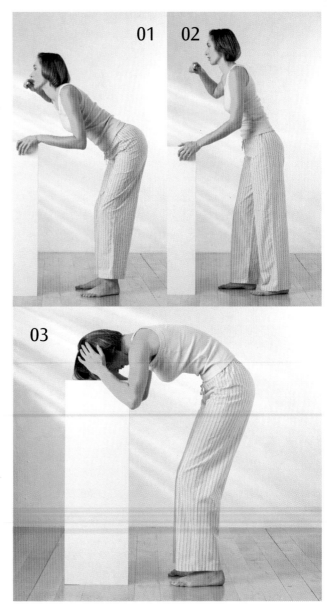

HAIR-BRUSHING

(04) Keep your back and knees straight and your stomach muscles drawn in. Don't throw your head back and hunch your shoulders to resist the pull of the brush.

PRACTISING BALANCE *(05)*

If you have trouble standing on one leg to put on socks, try this easy exercise.

(05) Breathe in, and as you breathe out, take your weight on one leg, in the centre of the foot. Lift the other knee, resting your hand on your thigh. Feel your leg stretch. Swap legs.

STANDING COSSACK

(01–02)
To loosen the back and improve overall flexibility.

(01) Stand with feet parallel, slightly apart. Clasp your forearms in front of you, away from your body.

(02) Breathe in, and as you breathe out, turn your upper body to the left. Breathe in, and as you breathe out, return to centre. Repeat for the right-hand side.

ARM ROTATION

To release the shoulder and improve joint mobility. This is an excellent exercise if you suffer from restricted shoulder movement.

(01) Stand sideways on to the hand basin and hold on to it with one hand. Have your feet apart and one just in front of the other. The front leg should be slightly bent. With a soft, easy back (drawing your stomach muscles in) lean down and let one hand hang loosely. Feel the weight of your arm. Breathe in, and as you breathe out, make stirring, circling movements with your hand. Repeat for the other hand.

PILATES REMINDERS
■ *Keep your stomach muscles pulled in throughout the exercise*
■ *Use the in-breath to prepare*
■ *Use the out-breath to make the action*

01

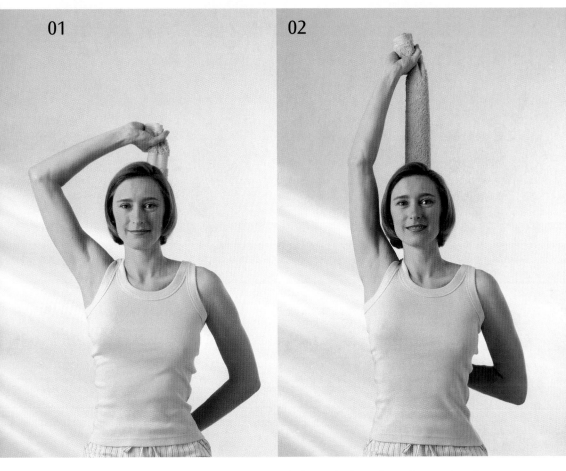

01

02

***TOWEL STRETCH** (01–02)*
To loosen up your shoulders, making it easier to reach back fastenings.

(01) Grasp a hand towel behind you, an end in each hand. Breathe in, and as you breathe out, pull the towel down with your left hand.

(02) Breathe in again, and as you breathe out, pull the towel upward with your right hand. Breathe in and return to your starting position. Repeat the cycle 10 times.

01

02

AT BREAKFAST
While you are sitting at the breakfast table, check your posture.

SITTING POSTURE
(01) Sitting slumped like this is a bad way to start your day. Shoulders are hunched and feet pigeon-toed.

(02) Sit with your buttocks back, your thighs at right-angles, and your back straight. Draw your stomach muscles in. Have both feet flat and parallel. Rest your hands on your thighs. Try a few pelvic floor exercises (see p.129).

SHOULDER SHRUGS *(03–04)*
To release tension in your upper back.

(03) Let your arms hang loosely and have your knees slightly apart and feet parallel. Make sure your shoulders are relaxed. See also Step (05).

(04) Breathe in as you shrug your shoulders upward. Breathe out as you lower them. Do this 3 or 4 times.

ARM PRESSES *(05–06)*
To flex your lats and improve your posture while sitting down. Keep your stomach muscles drawn in.

(05) With arms hanging by your sides, palms facing slightly outward, breathe in.

(06) As you breathe out, pull your left arm back as far as it will go, but without straining. Breathe in as you move your arm back again. Repeat in the same way for your right arm. Do 4 on each side.

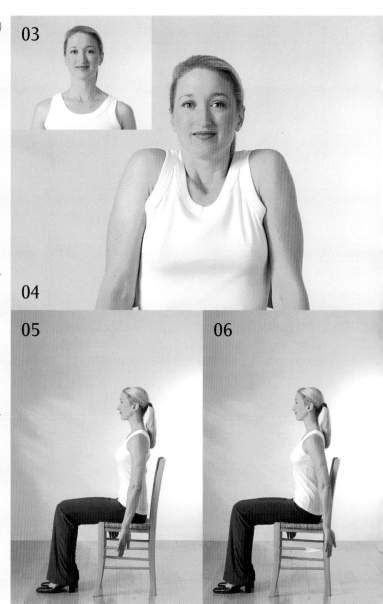

03
04
05
06

THE COSSACK

(07) Hold your folded arms out in front of you. Elongate your spine and hold your stomach muscles in. Feel the weight of your shoulder blades pulling down.

(08) Breathe in, and as you breathe out, turn to your right. Breathe in as you return to the centre. Repeat for the other side. Do the exercise 4 times on each side

AT THE KITCHEN SINK
(01–04)
Use odd moments at the sink to improve your posture.

BUTT SQUEEZE

(01) Stand up straight, pressing your hands down, and rotate your feet outward slightly. Breathe in, and on the out-breath, draw your stomach muscles in, squeezing your buttock muscles together.

RAISE HEELS

(02) With feet parallel, breathe in. As you breathe out, raise your heels, then gently lower them down again. Repeat 10 times.

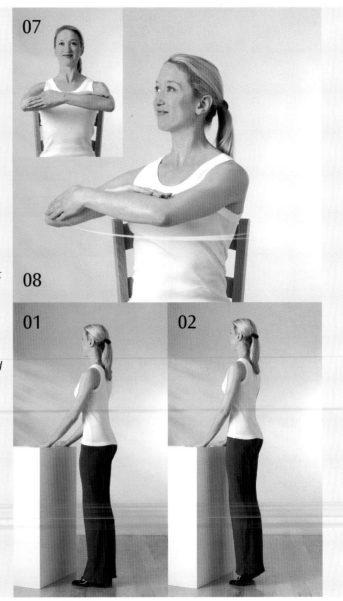

HAMSTRINGS

(03) Bend your left leg and extend the right. Breathe in, and as you breathe out, pitch your upper body forward, back straight. Feel your hamstrings stretching. Swap legs and repeat.

SIDE-STRETCHES

(04) With your right hand holding the sink and the other stretched up, breathe in. As you breathe out, bend your right knee and lean away, stretching your left arm over your head. Repeat for the other side.

PILATES REMINDERS

★ *Keep your stomach muscles drawn in throughout*
★ *Use the in-breath to prepare*
★ *Use the out-breath to make the action*

CHAPTER THREE

Travelling with Pilates

Most of us travel for both work and leisure, and although getting from place to place should be straightforward, it can be an uncomfortable, stressful experience. But help is at hand. Pilates is a highly "portable" exercise system that you can use any time, any place, to relieve travel stress and discomfort.

Whether you are taking a short walk to the local shops, or are on a long-haul flight to the other side of the globe, there are myriad ways in which Pilates can help you to make this aspect of your life easier, more comfortable, more safe, and also less stressful. In this chapter we look at the most commonly used means of travel: walking, car travel, train travel, and plane travel.

When you are taking a simple walk, a few moments' concentration and simple awareness, especially when you are carrying heavy bags, can prevent postural problems developing. Being in a car, perhaps stuck in a traffic jam, can give you a few spare moments to spend doing relaxing shoulder rolls and shrugs, and when you take a longer break, doing a few Pilates stretches can make all the difference to a long journey. Travelling by train can be frustrating, but adopting good posture when standing in a swaying train will help compose you and keep you occupied during any unexpected delays. And on a long plane journey there are several useful Pilates exercises you can do to keep your circulation going as well as your sanity intact.

Finally, we suggest a useful Pilates Hotel Routine that you can do in your hotel room. This will help keep you grounded while you are away from home and will also help to prepare and calm you if you have to attend important meetings or functions. No special equipment or clothes are necessary; you can simply make use of any props and furniture that are readily to hand.

Walking

Walking is the healthiest way of getting around and a good, brisk walk, lasting about 15 minutes, several times a week and if possible every day, will keep you fit and healthy. Whatever the distance you are covering, it is important to wear comfortable, supportive shoes with low heels that you feel confident about walking distances in. Platforms, backless shoes, high heels, and clogs are not a good choice. If you have to wear elegant, delicate shoes for work, then carry them with you and wear another pair for the journey. Your shoes should allow your foot to articulate fully, with soles that are not too thick or inflexible, otherwise the muscles in your lower leg will suffer unnecessary strain.

If you are carrying bags of books or shopping, be careful how you do it. It is all too easy to damage your back or shoulders by repeatedly carrying heavy bags that weigh you down on one side. A properly adjusted backpack, using both straps not just one, is probably the best solution of all.

GENERAL SELF-HELP
- Make the most of the thousands of steps that you take every day, to improve your overall fitness levels.
- Take a good, brisk walk for about 15 minutes per day to keep fit and fully exercised.
- Get off the bus or train a stop early in order to get a good walk every day.

WALKING POSTURE
As you take a step, be conscious of using the whole foot, "walking through" from the heel to the toes. Your centre of gravity should come down through the front of your heel.

01

02

CARRYING BAGS

(01) Avoid carrying a single heavy bag. This causes tension in the elbow and neck. The hips are off-centre and strain is transferred to the lower back. If you cannot split the load, change sides frequently.

(02) Carry two equally weighted bags, so that the body is balanced. Or use a backpack, with both straps.

In the car

Different makes of car have different styles of adjustable seat. Check that your seat is at the correct height and angle for you and the correct distance from the foot controls. Make sure that you can see in the rear view mirror without stretching, leaning, or moving your head. Avoid twisting your body to reach into the back seat and keep both hands on the wheel. You might find that using a backrest relieves strain on the lumbar spine, reducing the risk of back problems. On a long journey, take regular breaks (every two hours at least) to restore concentration and stretch out tension in the shoulders, hips, and spine muscles. If you can, swap drivers to get a proper rest.

STUCK IN TRAFFIC (01–05)
With the brake on and the gear in neutral, sit with your buttocks fitting into the back of the seat and your back fully supported.

(01) Breathe in, and as you breathe out, shrug your shoulders up toward your ears. Repeat 10 times.

(02) Breathe in. As you breathe out, draw your stomach muscles in. Hold for a count of 4. Relax. Try some pelvic rocking. Holding the wheel with both hands, lengthen the spine, and rock the pelvis gently, first forward and then back. Then do some pelvic floor exercises (see also p.129) by pulling the pelvic floor up toward the ribcage.

(03–5) Now, still holding the wheel with both hands, try some relaxing forward shoulder rolls. Breathe in, and as you breathe out, circle your shoulders forward and then backward (not shown). Bring them round to the front again. Repeat 10 times.

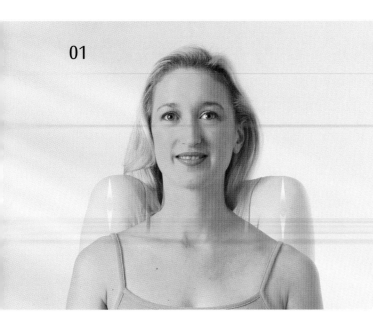

01

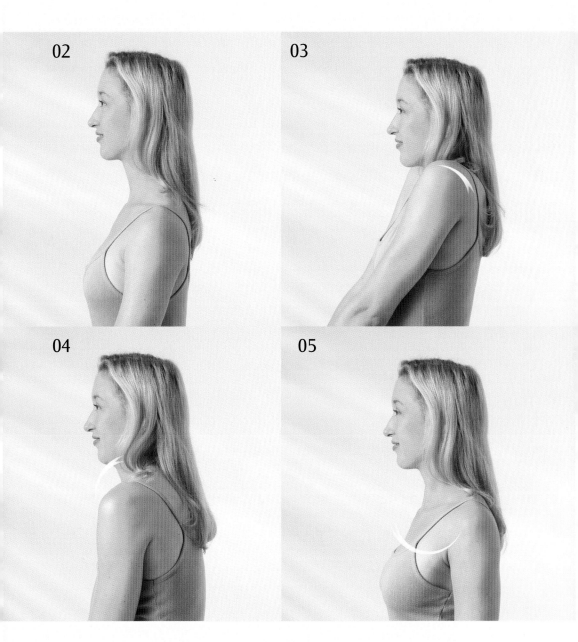

01

02

RESTING FROM DRIVING

Do not attempt to drive for more than 2 hours without taking a proper rest. Stop in a designated stopping place and get out of the car and walk around to stretch your legs. If possible, have a snack and a non-alcoholic drink or a cup of coffee. If you can, take a short nap (10 to 15 minutes).

CAT STRETCHES

(01) Holding on to the side of the car, try some cat stretches. Keeping your thighs together and your stomach in, breathe in, curve your spine, and drop your head down.

(02) As you breathe out, arch your back and bring your head up again.

03

04

CALF STRETCHES
(03) With hands on the side of the car, place your right leg in front of your left, with your knee bent and the heel on the ground. Breathe in, and on the out-breath, gently lean forward, feeling the stretch in the back of your left calf. Repeat for the other leg.

HAMSTRING STRETCHES
(04) Hold the side of the car with one hand, cross your left leg over your right, keeping both straight. Hold your left leg with your left hand and curve your torso over, dropping your head right down. Breathe in, and as you breathe out, feel the stretch in the backs of your legs. Swap legs and repeat.

Train travel

Train travel can be an unpleasant experience. Trains are frequently overcrowded, with nowhere to sit and long, unexpected delays. Use the time to do some Pilates exercises. If you have to go up an escalator at the station, use the opportunity to do some aerobic exercises and calf stretches.

If you are fortunate enough to get a seat, sit with both feet squarely on the floor and do not be tempted to cross your legs (see also the sitting posture on page 50). Sit well into the back of the seat so that your back is fully supported. Draw your stomach muscles in. Have your shoulders relaxed. If you do have to stand, hold on to a solid handrail and try to relax into the rhythm of the train. Don't try to brace yourself and resist the movement. Put your hand luggage somewhere secure. If you have to stand holding a bag, swap it from one hand to the other at regular intervals.

GENERAL SELF-HELP
- Don't be tempted to stand slouched on one hip (see 01, top right).
- Have both feet firmly planted on the ground (see 02, right), so that your weight is evenly distributed. Keep your knees straight, but not locked. Gently squeeze your buttock muscles for extra balance and draw your stomach muscles in.
- To relax, put one foot in front of the other, with the front knee slightly bent and the back knee straight. Keep your hips square.

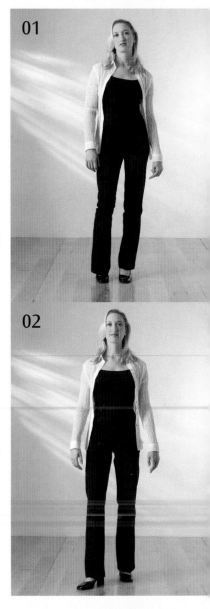

01

02

Plane travel

Travelling by plane is usually the most efficient means of covering distances quickly and is used by millions of people every day both for short- and long-haul journeys, business and pleasure. But flying comes with a serious health warning attached. Use Pilates and the general self-help advice below to minimize the side effects of air travel and make your trip as comfortable and enjoyable as possible. Pilates exercises can help you overcome the problems associated with sitting still in a confined space for long periods. One of the biggest health risks is deep vein thrombosis (DVT). This is caused by your circulation slowing due to inactivity and blood stagnating in certain areas, particularly the legs, and forming clots. If the clot circulates to the heart or brain, this can prove fatal (see also p.69).

GENERAL SELF-HELP

- Drink plenty of plain water to keep hydrated and replace lost fluids. Alcohol may help you relax, but it is a diuretic and will cause further dehydration. Take your own 2-litre (3-1/2 pint) bottle of water with you.
- Avoid eating salty snacks and "junk" food as salt encourages water retention, which can make your feet, legs, and ankles swell and your eyes puffy. Take a banana and a bag of unsalted nuts to have instead.
- Wear flat shoes and loose-fitting clothes. Tight waistbands restrict breathing and circulation.
- Take a mister and spray your face at intervals to stop your skin becoming dry.
- Walk around the plane every couple of hours.

SITTING CORRECTLY
(unillustrated – see p.50)
Sit in your seat with both feet flat on the floor. If you have long legs, ask for an aisle seat. Don't be tempted to cross or curl up your legs as this will impede good circulation. Sit up straight so that your spine is not crunched up and your weight is evenly balanced on both buttocks. Keep your shoulders relaxed. Draw your stomach muscles in and do some pelvic floor exercises (see p.129).

01

02

USING THE PLANE SEAT (01–06)
Get up and go to the back of the plane. Find
an unoccupied seat. If there isn't one, ask the
occupant's permission first.

(01) Hold the back of a seat, with knees bent.

(02) Drawing your stomach in, keeping your
back straight and knees bent, breathe in, and
rise up on to your toes. Hold for a few seconds.

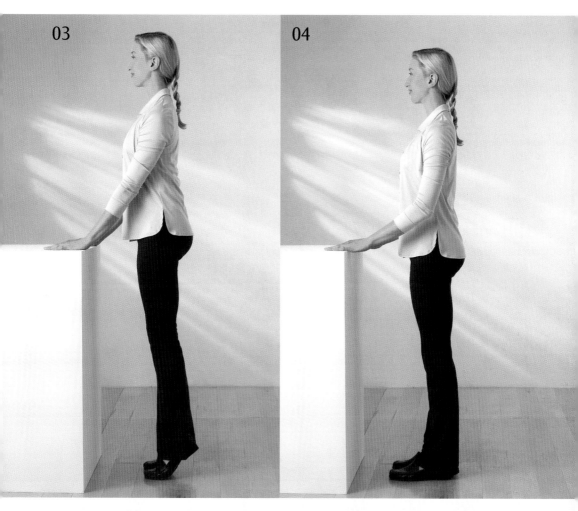

(03) Breathe out and straighten your knees, remaining on tiptoes.

(04) Breathe in and lower again on to flat feet, keeping your back straight and making sure your tailbone is directed toward the floor. Repeat the sequence 10 times.

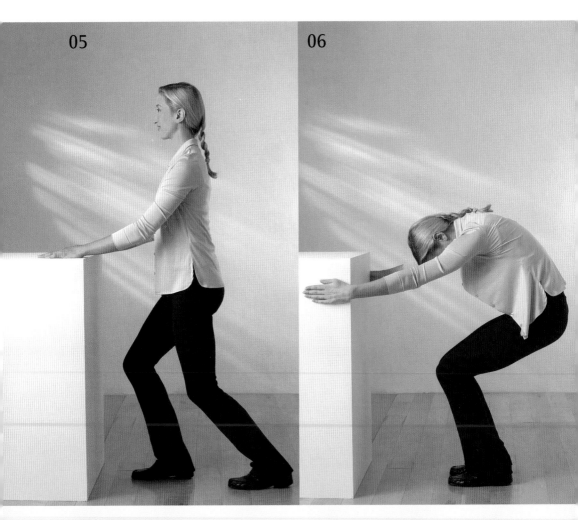

05

06

CALF STRETCHING
(05) *Place one leg behind the other, breathe in, and as you breathe out, bend your back knee, keeping your back straight. Feel the stretch in your back calf. Hold for 5 seconds.*

LOWER BACK STRETCH
(06) *With legs and feet together, holding on to the back of the seat, breathe in, and as you breathe out, bend to a semi-squat. Breathe in and return to the starting position.*

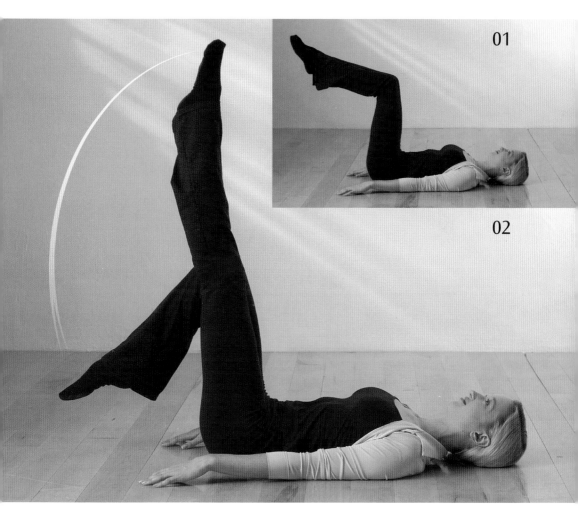

CIRCULATION BOOSTER

(01–02) Lie down at the back of the plane or in the aisle, making sure that you do not cause an obstruction or inconvenience others. Place your arms by your sides and draw your stomach muscles in. Breathe in, and as you breathe out, lift your legs, keeping your knees together. Now kick your legs alternately, as rapidly as you can, until they get tired, making sure that your knees stay together.

01

SHOULDER CIRCLES AND NECK STRETCHES

If you have room on either side of you while you are sitting in your seat, place your fingertips on your shoulders. If not, rotate your shoulders with your hands on your thighs.

CIRCLES (unillustrated)

Take your shoulders up toward your ears and then circle them back and downward.

STRETCHES (01)

If you are travelling with a partner, try the exercise on page 123, but if you are on your own try these solo neck stretches. Keep your neck long and your shoulders relaxed throughout.

Gently place your head to one side, then back to the centre again. Then place your head to the other side. Repeat several times. To flex your neck more, incline your head on each side as well (as shown here), making sure your shoulders remain still.

FOOT WAGGLING AND CIRCLING

It is vital to keep the circulation flowing in your ankles and lower legs.

(01) To waggle your feet, sit right back in your seat and if there is space, put a pillow under one thigh, just above the knee. Flex the foot up and then down again. Repeat for the other foot.

(02) Circle your feet in both directions, repeating 10 times for each foot.

FLIGHT SOCKS

Try wearing a pair of special elasticated flight socks. These work by exerting varying amounts of pressure on different parts of the leg, so that increased blood flows back to the heart. This can help to prevent blood clots (DVT). The socks are particularly good if you are over 40 and if your flight lasts longer than 4 hours.

WARNING

Do not wear these socks if you suffer from arterial disease or diabetes.

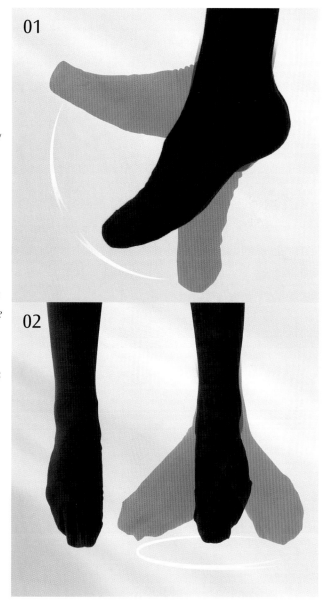

01

02

In your hotel room

Some people find travelling stressful and being away from home an unsettling experience. If you are already carrying out a regular Pilates exercise routine at home (see pp.39–43 or 89–101), try this specially designed hotel routine to help you adjust to being away from home and get you through any challenging situations you may have to confront.

You can do the Pilates Hotel Routine whenever it suits you during the day. If you are too rushed in the morning, do it in the evening, either before you go out or before retiring for the night. If you are on a business trip, you can do it to calm and centre yourself before attending an important meeting, or even before making a difficult phone call.

01

PILATES HOTEL ROUTINE
(01–25)

THE CAT *(01–02)*
To mobilize the spine and work the stomach muscles. Get on to all-fours, with your shoulders and hips in a straight line. It may be necessary to adjust your arm position to maintain the natural curve of the spine.

(01) As you breathe in, starting the movement from your pelvis and stomach, curve your spine toward the ceiling, allowing your head to dip toward the floor.

(02) Then breathe out, gently dropping your back into an arch, supported by the stomach muscles. Make sure your arms are straight, your shoulders relaxed, and your neck long. Repeat 10 times.

REST POSITION
(03) Sit back on your heels and rest your forehead on the floor, stretching your arms out in front. Remain in this position for up to 3 minutes, breathing deeply.

02

03

ABDOMINAL CURLS *(04–05)*
To strengthen all the stomach muscles.

(04) Start in a sitting position, holding your arms parallel to the floor. You may want to tuck your feet under a piece of furniture for support.

(05) Breathe in, and as you breathe out, slowly lower yourself to the floor, using your abdominals to control your curve-down. Feel your coccyx sliding toward your heels. If you run out of breath take a quick in-breath and continue breathing out. Rest for a few seconds. Lift yourself back to the starting position, using your hands if necessary. As you get stronger, try to curl back to the starting position without using your hands or tensing your back.

04

05

06

07

OBLIQUES *(06–07)*

Important for supporting the pelvis and back and helping side-to-side turns.

(06) Lie on the floor and put your feet on the bed or on a chair or stool of suitable height. Rest your head on a pillow, placing your left hand behind your head and your right hand on your stomach.

(07) Breathe in, and as you breathe out, draw your stomach muscles in. Raise your upper torso and roll diagonally toward your left knee, reaching past it with your right hand. Return to the resting position. Then swap sides and repeat. Do the sequence about 10 times.

08

09

GLUT SQUEEZE (08–09)

To strengthen the gluts, helping to support the pelvis, strengthening the lower back.

(08) Lying on your back, feet flat on the floor, bend your knees to 90 degrees. Place your arms by your sides, palms down.

(09) Breathe in and gently, as you breathe out, without tilting the pelvis, raise your hips up and squeeze your buttock muscles together. Hold for a count of 4. Slowly lower again, releasing your buttock muscles and keeping your torso long and open. Repeat 10 times.

10

11

BUTT SQUEEZE

(10) Place a pillow under your stomach, resting forehead on hands. Breathe in, and as you breathe out, squeeze the buttock muscles together. Imagine your "sitting bones" pulling together. Hold for count of 4. Breathe in and relax. Repeat 10 times.

HAMSTRINGS

(11) Breathe in, and as you breathe out, slowly bend your left leg from the knee, toward your buttocks, to form a 90-degree angle. Keep your heel on a central line. Breathe in and lower the foot. Swap legs and repeat 10 times for each.

ADDUCTORS

To tone your inner thigh muscles.

(12) Sitting on the floor, against the side of the bed if you need more support, spread your legs wide and bend your right knee, holding it with your right hand. Flex your feet. Relax your shoulders and neck. Breathe in, and as you breathe out, slide your free leg toward the bent leg. Breathe in to return to the starting position. Do the exercise 10 times for each leg.

SHOULDER SHRUGS

To release the neck and shoulders.

(13) Sitting on a chair or stool, do some pelvic floor exercises (see p.129) and then do some simultaneous shoulder shrugs. Breathe in as you move your shoulders up, and out as you move them down.

SHOULDER CIRCLES

(14) Place your fingertips on your shoulders and do some shoulder circles. As you breathe in, circle your elbows forward and as you breathe out circle them backward (as shown). Imagine you are drawing circles with your elbows on a blackboard on either side.

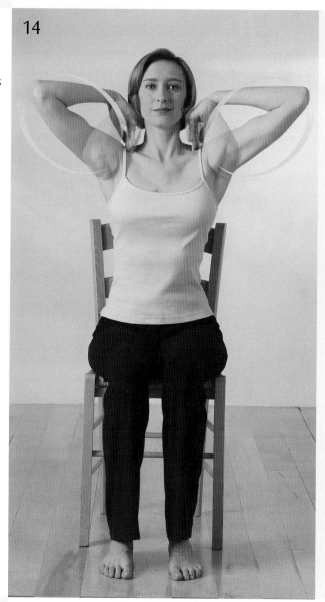

14

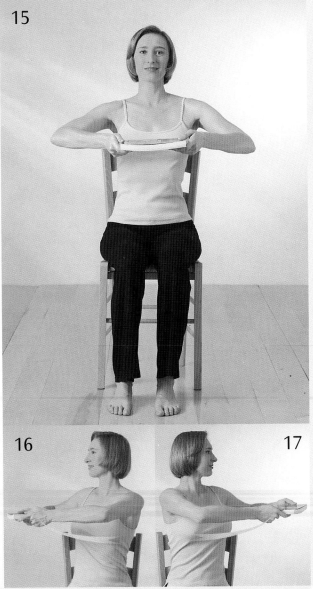

COSSACK

(15) Sitting down, hold a book in front of you, elbows away from your body.

(16) Breathe in, and as you breathe out, rotate the book to your right.

(17) Breathe in and return to centre. Breathe out to rotate the book to your left.

UPPER TORSO STRETCH

(18) Lie on your back, with knees up. Clasp your upper arms in front of you.

(19) Breathe in, and as you breathe out, bring your left elbow down to the floor on your left side. Breathe in, and on the out-breath, come back through the centre, and over to the other side. Continue from side to side.

(20) (continuation) Start as in Step (18). Instead of bringing your arms through the centre, circle them around the top of your head, as close to the floor as possible. Think of drawing a semicircle on the floor.

18

19

20

THE WINDMILL *(21–23)*
(21) Lying on your back, knees bent, back flat, stomach muscles gently pulled down to the floor, raise both arms up to the ceiling.

(22) Breathe in, and as you breathe out, stretch your right arm back above your head and lower your left arm to your side. Breathe in to bring both arms back to the vertical.

(23) Breathe out, lower your right arm to your side and bring your left arm above your head. Alternating arms, repeat the sequence 10 times.

HEEL ON WALL *(24–25)*
To stretch your hamstrings.

(24) Lie down and place one heel against a wall, holding a towel around it. As you breathe in, press your heel into the wall for a count of 4, raising your head, shoulders, and upper back off the floor. (Can be done without curving the upper torso forward.)

(25) As you breathe out, pull your heel away, keeping your leg straight, letting your upper torso, head, and shoulders gently back down to the floor. Swap legs and repeat 10 times for each leg.

CHAPTER FOUR

Pilates at work

Whatever kind of work you do, whether you are based at home or in an office, Pilates can help you strengthen and tone your body, using simple exercises that you can do any time of the day. Just take a few moments to focus on your breathing and posture, and you will feel more ready and able to carry out your work.

This chapter is divided into two main parts: the physical work we do in the home and the most common postures and physical situations we find ourselves in in the office.

The first part of the chapter tackles the sort of jobs you need to do in the home, such as vacuuming or taking heavy items out of the oven. Most people do these jobs in a hurry and are too rushed to take the time to think about how they are moving and manipulating things. It is all too easy to put yourself at risk by, for example, bending down while keeping your knees straight, when to have them slightly bent would be the safer, healthier option. The Pilates Housework Routine is suggested to help tone and strengthen all the parts of your body that you need to carry out all the commonest household tasks and prevent physical damage.

The second part of the chapter deals with office-based problems such as the dangers posed by repetitive strain injury, the postural difficulties caused by sitting in front of a computer screen for long periods, and using a phone handset safely.

There is also a useful Pilates Office Routine that you can do at the office, either alone or with a colleague as your partner. Swap over so that you can both take turns to be treated. These include a number of relaxing, stress-busting exercises using props, such as office chairs, desks, and bottles of drinking water, that are likely to be readily to hand.

Pilates for housework

The physical actions that jobs around the house involve fall into the main categories of bending, lifting, reaching, and the push–pull action. Many jobs in the home require a combination of all these movements. It is a normal reaction to carry out these actions in a rush, just to get the task done and move on to a more engaging activity. But unfortunately it is all too easy to injure yourself by, for example, lifting a heavy piece of furniture in the wrong way. However, if you take your time to do the job a little more mindfully, you can use Pilates to make any of these movements less potentially damaging to your body,

NORMAL VACUUMING
(01–02)
Try not to rush the job and employ slow, rhythmic strokes rather than sharp, aggressive ones.

(01) This is the wrong way to vacuum and many people damage their backs in this way. The back is bent over and hunched, causing a drift away from the natural centre line of the body. The legs are straight, adding to the strain.

(02) This is the correct way to vacuum. Bend one knee and support your weight on it. Use a whole-body movement rather than just an arm movement. Breathe in, and breathe out to push the appliance away from you. Draw your stomach muscles in. Breathe in and pull the attachment toward you again.

01

02

and easier to carry out by means of body strengthening and toning. You will also enjoy doing the job more and be benefiting from exercise.

VACUUMING (CYLINDER MODELS)
This job involves a combination of bending, pushing, and pulling. You have to apply pressure to push the attachment along the carpet and you may have to bend down low to vacuum under furniture. Cylinder models are harder to manipulate than upright versions because the natural reaction is to bend the back in order to be able to apply enough pressure.

VACUUMING UNDER FURNITURE
(03) When you need to vacuum under low furniture, such as beds, don't be tempted to bend right over, with your knees straight and your head down.

(04) Squat down or bend one knee. Breathe in, and as you breathe out, push the appliance away from you, drawing your stomach muscles in. Breathe in as you pull the attachment back toward you again.

03

04

MOVING FURNITURE

If you are on your own, don't move anything that is too heavy to manage without straining. Wait until you can get someone to help you. If you can manage on your own, don't lean down, but squat or go on one knee. Use both hands and move slowly.

REACHING

If you can't reach the object with your feet flat on the floor, then it is too high. Don't be tempted to stretch any further. Get a small, lightweight step ladder or steady stool to stand on. Make sure that the item is not

LIFTING A HEAVY BOX

Don't tackle the task by leaning over with legs straight and a rounded back. Breathe in, and as you breathe out, bend your knees, grasping the box in both hands. Keep your back straight and your stomach muscles in. Breathe in, and as you breathe out, straighten your legs, keeping your back straight and your body weight along the centre line.

MOVING A TABLE

(not illustrated)
Do not try to move a table on your own. This job needs at least two people. Don't lean over with rounded back and straight legs. Bend your knees, keep your back straight and your body weight along the centre line. Breathe out to lift, pulling your stomach muscles in.

too heavy to lift down without bending over backward and losing your balance. If you are removing several separate objects from a high cupboard, try to avoid lifting them down all at once. Split things up into batches and climb up and down several times.

LIFTING FROM A LOW OVEN

When you are taking a heavy casserole out of a low oven, you are dealing with a potentially dangerous situation. Go slowly, even if you have to keep diners waiting, and wear thick oven mitts. Check that you have a firm grasp of both the casserole and its lid.

IRONING (01–02)

Make sure that the ironing board is the right height and that you do not have to twist in order to reach things. If you are feeling tired, lower the board and sit to iron.

(01) This ironing board is too low. The back is bent and the shoulders and torso are hunched uncomfortably, providing too much downward pressure. The neck and hands are tense. This makes it harder to move the iron.

(02) When adjusted to the correct height, body weight is distributed comfortably and the back is straight, shoulders relaxed. Your left leg should be slightly turned outward. Hold your stomach muscles in.

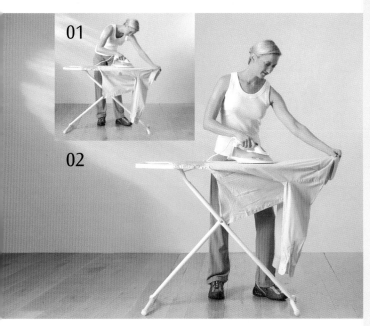

01

02

Making housework easier

The Pilates Housework Routine on the next few pages (pp.88–101) includes all the exercises you need to strengthen and tone your body, to make all the main household tasks easier and safer to carry out. Take a break from the chores and fit the routine in at any time of the day – whenever it's convenient for you.

GENERAL SELF-HELP
- Wear loose, comfortable clothes.
- Take time to do household jobs mindfully. Don't be tempted to rush just to get your tasks done.
- Pilates helps strengthen the appropriate muscles.

PILATES REMINDERS
- *Keep your stomach muscles pulled in throughout*
- *Use the in-breath to prepare*
- *Use the out-breath to make the action*

01

PILATES HOUSEWORK ROUTINE (01–32)

You don't have to do this routine all at once. Don't let it become a chore like the housework: break it up into smaller chunks.

ABDOMINAL CURL (01–02)

This exercise will help strengthen your abdominals. Having strong abs helps you to support your back, whatever task you are doing in the home.

(01) Lie on your back with your knees raised and a rolled-up towel or paperback book beneath your head. Put a small cushion between your knees to make you use your inner thighs and keep your pelvis stable. Let your upper body remain relaxed and release any tension. Put both hands on your thighs.

(02) Breathe in, and as you breathe out, draw your stomach in. Gradually walk your fingers up your thighs, allowing your head and shoulders to curl off the floor. When you have reached as far as you can, breathe in again, and as you breathe out, draw in your stomach muscles and roll gently back down again. Do the sequence 10 times.

02

03

04

OBLIQUE SIT-UPS (03–04)
To stabilize the pelvis and the lower back, helping you to twist and turn safely as you carry out household jobs.

(03) Lie on your back with your knees raised and a cushion held between them. This makes you use your thighs while keeping your pelvis stable. Put a rolled-up towel or paperback book beneath your head. Place your hands behind your head, under your hairline. Raise your elbows off the floor.

(04) Breathe in, and as you breathe out, draw your stomach in. Curl your head and shoulders diagonally toward your left knee. Breathe in and return to the resting position. Repeat for the other side and do the whole sequence 10 times.

OBLIQUE SIT-UP VARIATION (05–06)
(05) Repeat Step (03), facing page.

(06) Breathe in, and as you breathe out, draw
your stomach in, curl your head and
shoulders diagonally toward your left knee.
Slowly take your right hand away from your
head and stretch it toward the knee, trying to
lift a little higher. Breathe in, place your right

hand back behind your head and return to
the starting position. Alternate sides 10 times.

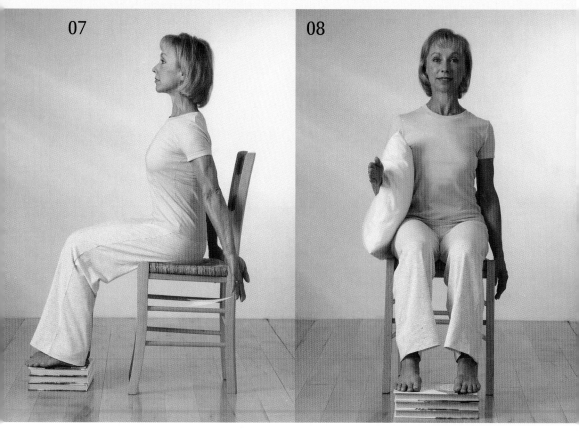

LATS STRENGTHENING (07–08)
To strengthen muscles below the shoulder blades and stabilize the upper torso.

(07) Sit on a chair or stool, arms relaxed at your sides, neck long, shoulders relaxed. Your feet should be flat, facing forward, thighs parallel. Breathe in, and as you breathe out, gently stretch your hands down, rotate your arms inward, and stretch them behind. Make sure that your torso remains in the same position. Repeat 10 times.

CUSHION-SQUEEZING (08)
Strengthens the middle to upper back, helping with jobs that involve stretching up.

(08) Place a cushion under your right arm. Breathe in, and as you breathe out, squeeze it. Swap and repeat 10 times each side.

SITTING SIDE-STRETCH
(09–10)
For all-round flexibility and fitness.

(09) Sit sideways-on, holding the chair back with your right hand. Your thighs should be parallel to the floor. If necessary, support your feet with a footstool or stack of books. Raise your left arm over your head, to make a soft curve. Keep your back straight and hold your stomach in.

(10) Breathe in. As you breathe out, incline your upper body toward your right, turning your head in the same direction. Make sure that you do not lean too far away from the chair. Breathe in as you return to centre. Repeat 4 times and then change to the other side.

09

10

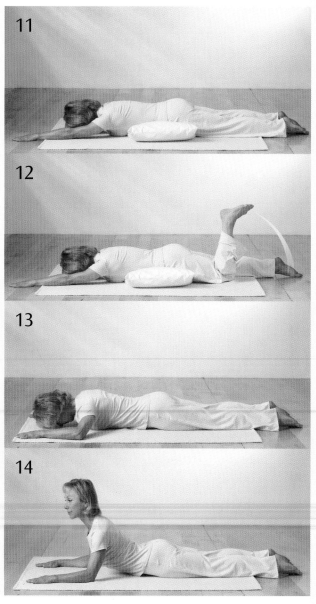

11

12

13

14

HAMSTRING CURL *(11–12)*
To strengthen the muscles that run from the back of the knee up to the buttocks.

(11) Lie on your front with a pillow beneath your stomach, resting your head on your right hand and stretching your left hand out.

(12) Breathe in, and as you breathe out, slowly bend your left leg to an angle of 90 degrees. Imagine your heel being pulled in a line toward your left hand. Breathe in as you lower your foot. Repeat 10 times for your left leg and then swap.

COBRA *(13–14)*
To strengthen the lower back muscles. (Don't overstretch.)

(13) Lie face down, without the cushion. Bend your arms, palms down. Gently squeeze the buttocks together.

(14) Breathe in, and as you breathe out, slowly raise your upper body off the ground, keeping your spine long and your arms in the same position. Breathe in, and return to the starting position. Repeat 10 times.

15

16

17

18

INNER THIGHS

(15) Lie on your left side, aligning your hips and shoulders. Place a cushion beneath your right knee and another between your head and left arm. Support your waist with a rolled-up towel. Stretch your left leg away from you.

(16) Breathe in, and as you breathe out, pull your abdominals in. Extend and lift your lower leg, your knee facing forward. Breathe in, and lower it again, keeping the whole movement smooth. Do this 10 times and repeat on the other side.

OUTER THIGHS

(17) Bend your left leg and place a large cushion beneath your flexed right foot. Rest your right hand on your hip.

(18) Breathe in, and as you breathe out, draw your abdominals in. Keeping your right leg parallel, lift it as high as possible, without moving your hips. Breathe in as you lower it again. Repeat 10 times on each side.

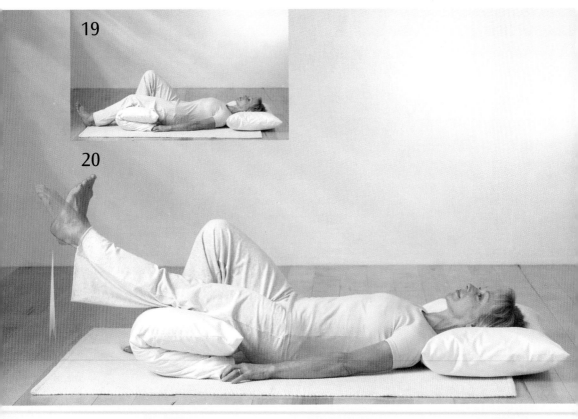

STRENGTHENING FRONT OF LEG (QUADRICEPS) (19–20)

To also work the calf muscles and help to strengthen and mobilize the ankle joints.

(19) Lie on your back, with your head and shoulders supported by a large pillow. Bend your left leg over another pillow, with the foot flexed. Bend your right knee and gently press the right foot into the floor. This helps to stabilize the pelvis during the exercise.

(20) Slowly lift your flexed foot until the leg is straight. Point the toe without bending your knee. Hold for a few seconds. Then flex the foot back and slowly lower it to the starting position. Repeat 10 times for each leg.

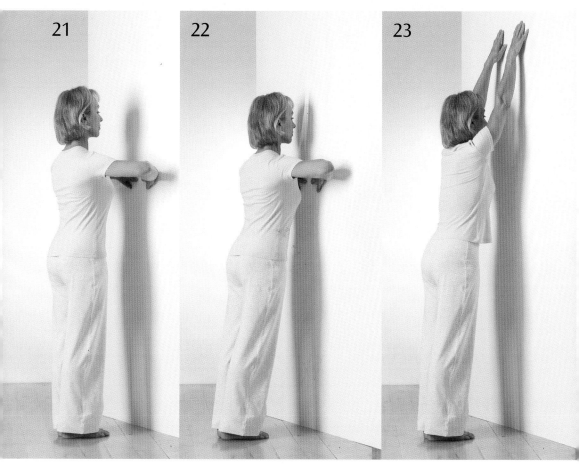

STRENGTHENING THE BACK

(21) Face a wall and keep your back straight. Put your inward-turned palms flat on the wall at shoulder-height, fingertips touching, elbows out. Depending on the length of your upper arms, you may need to separate your fingertips.

(22) Breathe in and lean in to the wall. Breathe out and return to starting position.

(23) Breathe in as you walk your fingers up, until your arms are stretched, without raising your shoulders. Breathe out and come back to the starting position. Repeat 10 times.

ARM STRENGTHENING (24–32)

If your muscles aren't toned and in good working order, placing too much pressure on a joint, such as when you are lifting heavy furniture, can cause ligament or joint problems.

PECTORALS (24–25)

(24) Lie on your back, with your knees up and feet flat on the floor, a hips'-width apart. Make sure that your back is in a natural position and that your neck and shoulders are relaxed. Holding a can in each hand, let your arms form a rounded shape, your hands level with your chest.

(25) Breathe in, and draw your stomach muscles in. As you breathe out, open your arms out to the sides, keeping them in the curved shape. Breathe in as you return to the starting position. Repeat 10 times. (This exercise can be done reversing the breath.)

TRICEPS *(26–27)*
Think of this exercise as "cosmetic", toning the backs of your arms.

(26) Still lying on your back, with knees raised and feet flat, stretch your left arm upward, holding the can, and place your right hand behind your elbow to steady it.

(27) Breathe in, drawing your stomach muscles in. Slowly lower your left hand toward your left shoulder. Breathe out and bring it back up slowly to the starting position. Repeat for the other side, holding the can in your right hand and supporting your right elbow with your left hand. Do the sequence 10 times.

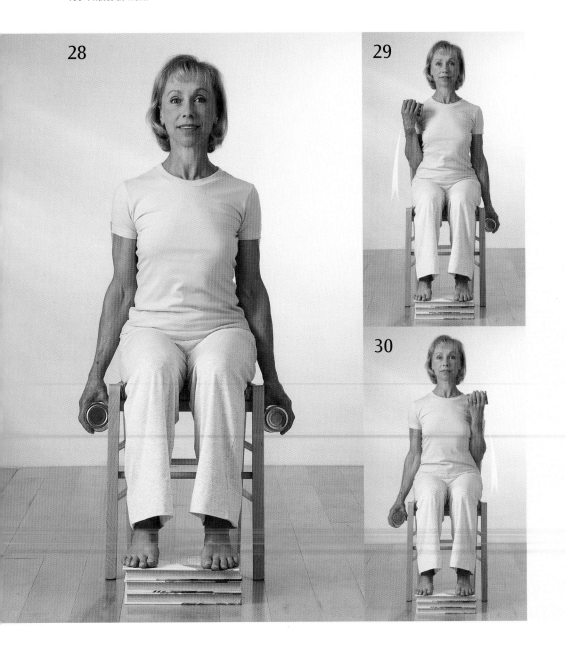

BICEPS *(28–30)*
(28) Sit on a chair or stool, holding a can in each hand. Support your feet.

(29) Breathe in, and as you breathe out, slowly turn your right hand and gently bend your right arm at the elbow to raise the can toward your shoulder. Breathe in and return to the starting position. Alternate arms 10 times on each side.

(30) As you feel more confident, raise and lower your arms in tandem.

DELTOIDS *(31–32)*
(31) Still sitting, and holding a can in each hand, allow your arms to hang down by your sides, palms facing in.

(32) As you breathe out, lift both arms out to the sides, as high as possible, without your shoulders moving. Breathe in and lower them to the starting position. Repeat 10 times.
  To make the exercise a little more difficult, position your hands slightly forward or backward from the vertical.

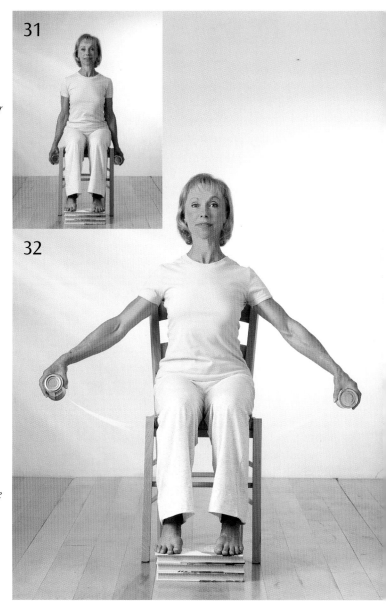

In the office

When you are working in an office there are several factors to take into consideration, to make sure that you remain fit and healthy. First, check that your chair is the right height for you. Second, make sure that your equipment, particularly your computer and its accessories, are arranged so that they do not cause you unnecessary strain. Third, take plenty of short breaks in the day to get up and walk around and do some quick Pilates exercises.

COMPUTER POSTURE

Position your screen straight on and not so that you have to twist your head or upper body to look at it. Its centre should be at eye level. Your keyboard should be straight in front of you and there should be plenty of space for your mouse and its mat. You should have enough room to manipulate your mouse and rest your forearm comfortably between movements. Don't be tempted to stare at the screen for long periods without pausing. Rest your eyes by looking out of the window regularly and change your posture and stretch. Do not remain seated in the same position for more than ten minutes. Ball chairs and back chairs can be a good option, but ordinary office chairs adjusted to the right height are probably the best choice. In spare moments take the opportunity to do some pelvic floor exercises (see p.129), making sure that your spine is fully extended. Imagine a string joining the top of your head to your pelvic floor muscles. Breathe in, and as you breathe out, imagine the string pulling your pelvic floor muscles gently upward. Release and repeat.

01

02

PHONE POSTURE
(01) Don't hold the phone in the crook of your neck. Longterm this can do great damage and even lead to crippling repetitive strain injury. Special hands-free frames are available.

(02) Hold the handset lightly and draw both shoulders down. Keep your back straight and wrist soft.

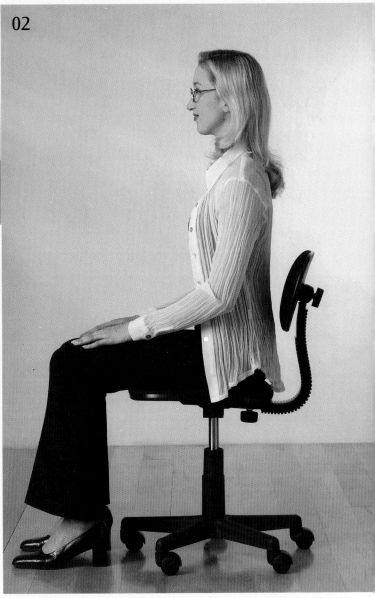

SITTING POSTURE

(01) Don't be tempted to sit with crossed legs or with them twisted around each other. This posture causes you to sit hunched forward.

(02) Sit with both feet flat on the floor, using a footstool if necessary. Your thighs should be at right-angles, fully supported. You should be able to lean forward from your hips with a straight back, allowing the arms to be free to work without tension.

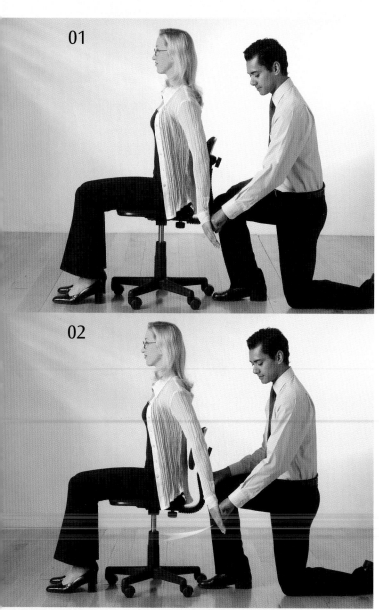

PILATES OFFICE ROUTINE
(01–26)
Ask a colleague to be your exercise partner for this routine, and then swap over so that you both have a turn.

INDIVIDUAL LAT PULLS
(01–02)
To strengthen the muscles that help to hold the shoulders and upper back in the correct postural position.

(01) Sit correctly in your office chair (see p.103). Let your arms hang by your sides. Ask your partner to make fists for your hands to press against.

(02) Breathe in, and as you breathe out, press your hands back against your partner's fists, as hard as you can. At the same time sit up straight and elongate the spine. Breathe in and return to the starting position. Repeat 10 times.

ASSISTED SHOULDER SHRUGS (03–04)
To help release shoulder and neck tension.

(03) Sit, with your partner holding your shoulders. Breathe in as your partner lifts your shoulders as high as possible.

(04) Breathe out as your partner pushes your shoulders gently back down again. Do this several times before rotating the shoulders backward and then forward.

ARMS OPENING (05–06)
To alleviate that hunched feeling and to open the shoulders and chest.

(05) Sit with feet flat on the floor. Relax your neck and shoulders. Hold your upper arms by your sides, at a 90-degree angle, palms facing.

(06) Breathe in, and as you breathe out, make a semicircle with your hands, keeping your upper arms close to your body. Breathe in, and return to the starting position. Repeat 10 times.

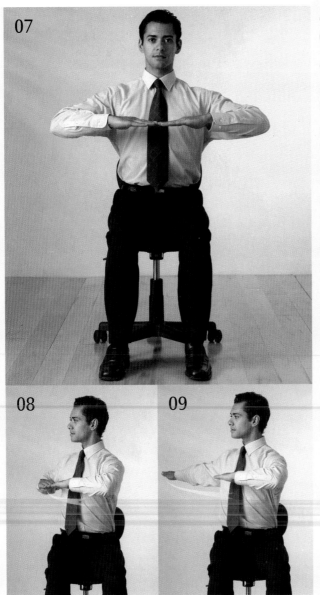

ONE-ARMED COSSACK
(07–09)
To help mobilize the middle of your back/thoracic spine.

(07) Sit with your fingertips touching, at chest height.

(08) Breathe in, and as you breathe out, rotate your upper body to the right. Pause.

(09) Breathe in, and as you breathe out, stretch one arm away and push it back as far as you can, rotating your body even more. Breathe in, bend your right arm, and return to the centre. Then do the same with your left arm on your left side. Repeat the sequence 10 times.

OPENING THE SHOULDERS

(10) Drop your head softly forward and cross your lower arms in your lap.

(11) Breathe in. As you bring your crossed arms up and over your head, imagine taking off a T-shirt. Arch your back, looking toward the ceiling.

(12) Stretch your arms and fingers into a wide V position. Breathe out as you circle your arms around and down to the starting position. Feel your shoulder blades pull down.

SITTING STATIC ABS

(not illustrated)
To strengthen the transverse abdominals.

Place your hands on your desk and both feet firmly on the ground. Breathe in. As you breathe out, pull your lats down, pressing your hands firmly onto the desk and draw the abdominal wall back toward your chair. To work the muscles harder, incorporate pelvic floor exercises (see p.129). Repeat 10 times.

10 11 12

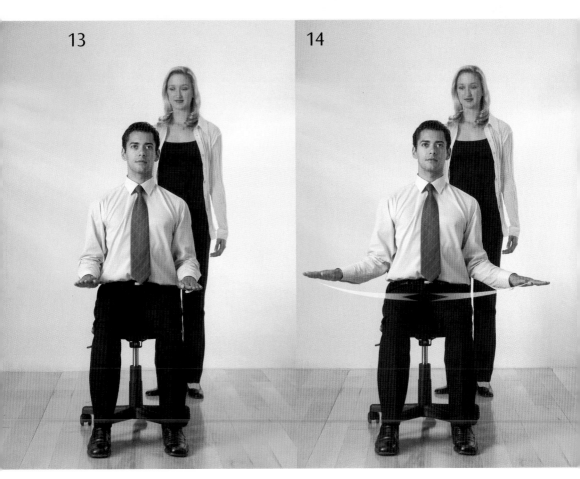

13

14

ELEVATED ARM OPENING *(13–16)*
For opening out the shoulders.

(13) Sit at your desk, with soft hands and palms facing down.

(14) Breathe in, and as you breathe out, move your arms out to the sides, as though opening a door. Breathe in and move them back to the centre again. Repeat the sequence 10 times.

(15) Breathe in, and as you breathe out, hold your arms out, palms facing down. For the next stage, rather than returning your arms to the starting position, breathe in and lift your elbows until your lower arms are parallel to the floor and your fingers are in line with your breast bone.

(16) Breathe in and move your arms back behind you. Your partner takes hold of your wrists and gently pulls your arms back. Breathe in as you return to the starting position – see Step (13), facing page.

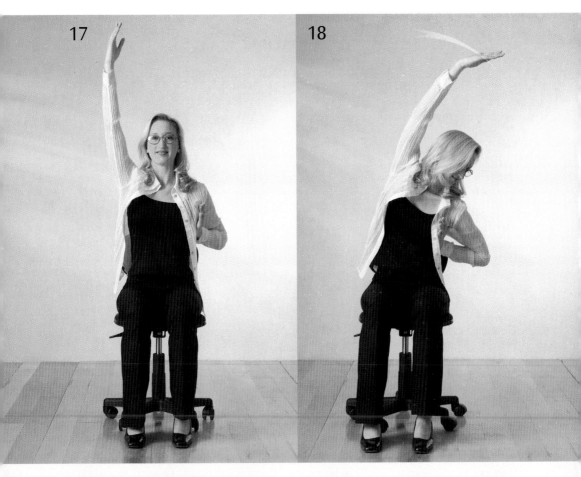

THORACIC SPINE SIDE-STRETCH (17–18)
To stretch the upper torso and open up the thoracic spine, which tightens when you are working on a computer.

(17) Position your hand tight into the ribs on your left side, close to the armpit, so that you are stabilized. Stretch your right arm up.

(18) Breathe in, and as you breathe out, stretch over to the left, curving the arm slightly and turning the head in the same direction. Breathe in and come back to the centre again. Repeat for the other side and do the sequence 10 times.

KNEE BEND WITH RISE *(19–21)*
To work the legs and stretch the calves.

(19) Kick your shoes off and stand behind your chair, holding its back with both hands. Breathe in, and as you breathe out, squeeze your buttock muscles together, pulling your stomach in, and relax.

(20) Breathe in and bend your knees.

(21) Breathe out and straighten your legs, lifting on to your toes. Breathe in and return to the starting position.

BUTT-LIFTER *(22–24)*
To tighten and lift the buttocks.

(22) Hold on to your chair with one hand, standing straight.

(23) Breathe in and lift your left leg. Hold it in your left hand.

(24) Take your knee out to your left side. Point your toe. On the out-breath make little lifts with your knee. Breathe in again and return to the centre. Repeat the sequence with the right leg. Do 4 on each side.

25

26

THE LUNGE (25–26)

To tone and condition your triceps and biceps. Keep your stomach in throughout and make sure that you do not lift your shoulder as you take your arm back. Hold a full water bottle to add weight.

(25) Stand behind your chair, with your right hand resting on the back. Place your right leg in front of the left. Bend the right leg so that you are leaning forward in a lunge.

(26) Breathe in, and as you breathe out, draw your stomach muscles in. Pull down your lats and bend your elbow to raise the bottle, keeping your elbow close to your waist. Take your arm back to the starting position and repeat 10 times on each side.

CHAPTER FIVE

Unwinding with Pilates

To get the most out of all aspects of your busy life and be able to survive and stay healthy, you need to learn how to make the most of your leisure time, too. The more you can get out of your down-time, the more you will be able to put in to your working activities, whether they are physical, mental, or a mixture of the two.

It is important to keep all aspects of our lives in balance. So when you get home from work, or if you work at home, make a conscious decision to switch to leisure mode: it is important to relax and let go of your day. If it has been stressful or unpleasant, then unwinding is even more vital. Then you will be able to recover your strength and energy and make the most of your evening.

It is vital to be able to enjoy the time you spend away from work, before returning to it the next day. It is all too tempting just to pour yourself a stiff drink and flop in front of the television. However, this may leave you feeling disgruntled and jittery by the time you go to bed. If you make a conscious effort to relax in a focused, creative way you will find that you can enjoy the evening more and feel more energized and positive when you wake up the following morning.

In this chapter we start off with a Pilates Unwinding Routine that you can do quickly, the moment you get home from work, or, if you work from home, when you move into "evening mode". Later you can try some relaxing and sensual massage and Pilates exercises with your partner, before getting ready for a good night's sleep.

It will help if you prepare yourself thoroughly for relaxation. Try burning relaxing aromatherapy oils and incense to create a calming atmosphere, play music that is special to you and which you find relaxing, and take the time to adjust the room lighting to create a relaxing mood. Candle light is perfect for this.

Releasing the day's stress

If you have been on the go all day long, and haven't had the chance to recharge your batteries along the way, here is a quick and easy Pilates routine to get you into a relaxed state of mind before you start the evening's activities.

GENERAL SELF-HELP
- Change out of your work clothes.
- Burn your favourite incense or calming aromatherapy oil, such as lavender.
- Light some candles for a relaxing atmosphere.
- Play some calming and uplifting music.

PILATES UNWINDING
ROUTINE (01–18)

KNEES TO CHEST (01–02)
To get rid of locked-in tension in your back and neck.

(01) Lie on your back, your whole spine in contact with the floor. Bend your knees, keeping them slightly apart and in line with your hips. Draw your stomach muscles in and hold throughout. Position your hands just below the knees.

((02) Breathe in, and as you breathe out, draw both knees down to your chest. Keep your spine on the floor and your neck long. Feel your back and chest opening out.

01

02

CLOCK FACE (03–06)
This exercise works on the entire lumbar region. The "clock" refers to the circle of the lumbar area, not to the circle that the knees make. Imagine you are lying on the clockface and that you are tracing a circle around the numerals.

(03) Lie on your back, with your whole spine stretched out and in contact with the floor. Place a paperback book under your head. Clasp your knees, gently pressing them together.

(04–06) Breathe in, and as you breathe out, draw your stomach muscles in and hold throughout. Using your hands to guide your knees, trace a small circle with them, but think about the larger circle that your back is making on the floor. Don't allow your hips to tip, and keep your movement small and subtle. Do 10 circles alternating clockwise and anticlockwise.

07

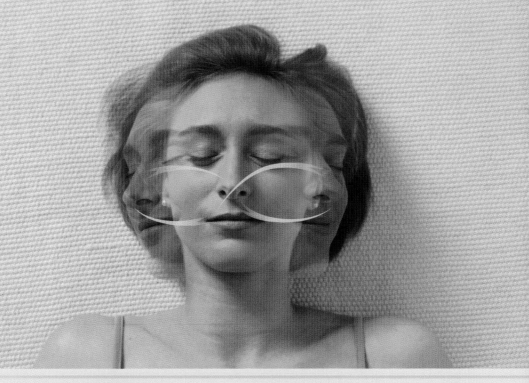

NOSE FIGURE-OF-EIGHT
This is a very subtle movement that involves close concentration (closing your eyes will help). As you are thinking about controlling your movement, the back of your neck relaxes. Lie on your back with your spine stretched along the floor, arms by your sides, and your knees bent. Draw your stomach muscles down. Hold this position throughout.

(07) Focus your attention on the tip of your nose and trace a figure-of-eight with it in the air. Make an almost imperceptible movement. Do 10 alternating figures-of-eight.

COSSACK SEMICIRCLES
(08–11)

To open out your upper back and shoulders. Don't be worried if you are unable to make a full circle at first. Your range will increase with practice.

(08) Lie on your back with your knees bent and your arms clasped in front of you in the cossack position. Hold your stomach muscles in throughout.

(09) Breathe in and take your joined arms over to your left side.

(10) Breathe out as you circle your clasped arms up over your head and around to the right side, then back into the starting position.

(11) Breathe in and take your arms over to your right side. Breathe out and circle around to the left. Come back to the centre again. Repeat the cycle 10 times.

08

09

10

11

12

13

14

LOWER BACK RELEASE
(12–14)
This is an excellent exercise if your lower back is tense and over-used.

(12) Lie on your back with your feet and knees together. Stretch your arms on to the floor behind you, hands overlapping.

(13–14) Breathe in, and as you breathe out, rock your knees from side to side as many times as possible on the outward breath. Stretch your arms right out. Repeat the sequence 8 times. It is nice to finish this exercise by bringing your knees up toward your chest – see p.116, Step (02).

DOMING *(15–16)*
This exercise "wakes up" your feet.

(15) Sit on a chair, with your knees at right-angles and your feet flat on the floor.

(16) Draw your toes back so that your instep lifts while your heel remains in contact with the floor. Try not to let your toes curl under. Hold the lift for a few seconds before straightening out your toes and returning to your starting position. Repeat 10 times for each foot.

FOOT MASSAGE
(17) Now try a foot massage. This is very good if you are prone to cramping. Gently stroke the whole foot. Then apply firmer pressure to the top of each toe, stretching it gently away from its base.

RELAXATION
(18) Lie with your legs against a wall, making sure that your feet are higher than your heart. Close your eyes and breathe gently. If possible relax for 5 minutes.

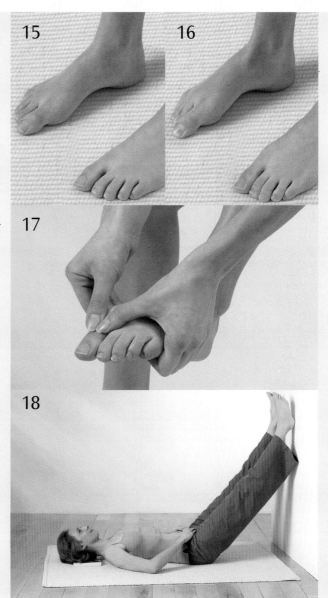

Partner work

Try some relaxing Pilates pair work with your partner, to complete your unwinding routine. This is a calming and harmonious way to end the day and is particularly important around the head and shoulder areas, where the accumulated tension of the day tends to get stored and trapped. You don't have to be an expert in massage to be able to help your partner relax – just trust in your natural healing skills. Swap roles, so that both of you can have a turn.

PILATES PARTNER ROUTINE (01–10)

SHOULDER STRETCH

(01) Hold your partner's elbows while he clasps his hands behind his neck. Resist with your hands as he tries to bring his elbows together.

(02) As your partner breathes out, use your forearms to lift his arms up and open, stretching him back. Hold for a second or two before returning to the starting position. Repeat 4 times.

01

02

SHOULDER MASSAGE

(03) Stand behind your seated partner, with your hands on his shoulders, thumbs at the back and fingers toward the front. Gently rotate your thumbs, first in one direction and then in the other. Gradually work away from the centre. Your partner should keep his head up and breathe easily and naturally.

NECK STRETCH

(04) With your left hand on your partner's shoulder, to add stability, and your right on the side of his head, gently stretch his head over to one side. Repeat on the other side.

(05) Turn your partner's head. Keep your left hand on his shoulder and place your right hand over the crown of his head. Gently stretch downward. The breathing should be easy and natural throughout. Repeat 2 to 3 times on each side.

03

04

05

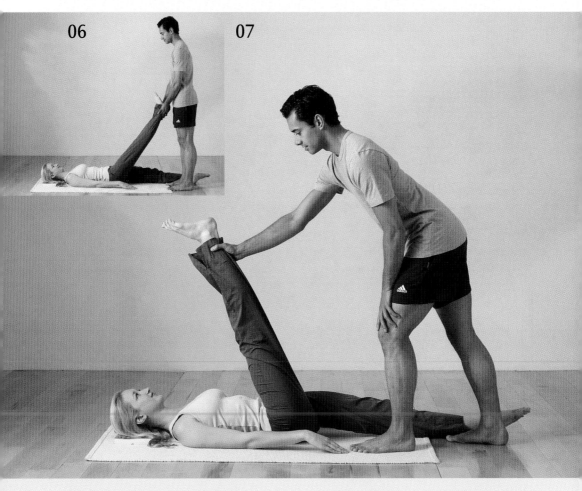

06

07

HAMSTRING STRETCH (06–07)
To make the hamstrings long and supple.

(06) Hold your partner's right leg at the ankle (both hands). As she breathes in, she presses her heel into your hand.

(07) On her out-breath, hold the leg with your left hand and gently stretch it toward the chest, shifting your weight onto your bent front leg. Stretch carefully, concentrating on your partner's reaction. Do not overstretch. Do 4 each side.

08

BACK STRETCH *(08–10)*
To stretch out the back

(08) Lie on the floor face down.

(09) Breathe in, and as you breathe out, lift up into the cobra position. Breathe in and return to the starting position. Repeat 4 times.

(10) On the fourth time lift up and slide back on to your hands and knees into the rest position (see also p.41). Your partner gently stretches your back by placing one hand between your shoulder blades and the other on the base of your back. Hold for a few seconds. Do this 4 times.

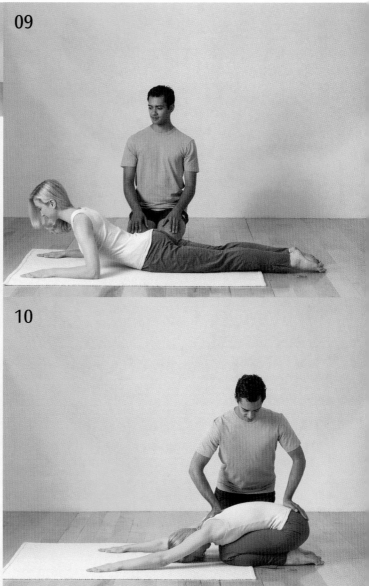

09

10

CHAPTER SIX

Pilates for pregnancy

Whether you are pregnant now, have already had your baby, or are planning one soon, Pilates supports and strengthens your body throughout and helps you stay healthy. Note which exercises can be done in early pregnancy and which must be avoided once your baby has grown into a pronounced bump.

Pilates is an excellent form of exercise if you are pregnant, as it is a low-impact exercise that will strengthen your back, stomach, and pelvic floor muscles. Keeping these muscles toned will not only help prevent backache, commonly associated with the latter stages of pregnancy but will also help your body recover more quickly after the birth. Your stomach will return more promptly to its natural shape. The way you control your breathing when you do Pilates will also help you breathe properly throughout labour and birth.

If you normally lead a sedentary lifestyle and don't exercise more than twice a week, consult your doctor before starting the Pilates exercises in this chapter. At the beginning, exercise only two or three times a week, for 15 to 20 minutes at a time. You can gradually increase the amount you do. Avoid overheating or exercising in hot conditions and always ensure that you drink plenty of water to avoid dehydration. Similarly, your body will need even more calories when you exercise during pregnancy, so always keep a healthy snack to hand.

In general, take everything more easily than you might otherwise and avoid all movements that are jerky or bouncy. For example, you should not participate in contact sports after the first 16 weeks of pregnancy. Try also to avoid fully flexing or hypertensing your joints. The most important thing is to listen to your body's needs: if you get tired when you are exercising, this is a strong signal to stop. Don't push yourself beyond your limits.

Pilates for life

You can do Pilates from before conception, right through to after the baby is born. Be aware that you should not lie on your front after your pregnancy has advanced by about two months and the baby has become a visible bump. After the first 30 weeks of pregnancy you should not lie flat on your back, because of the uncomfortable pressure of the growing baby on your internal organs. You should do the pelvic floor exercises well before pregnancy, and at all stages during and after the birth. It is a very good idea to carry on doing them right throughout your life, in fact, as they will stand you in good stead in later years, when your pelvic floor muscles begin to lose strength.

DON'T EXERCISE WITH:
- *Diabetes, thyroid, cardiovascular, respiratory, or renal diseases*
- *History of miscarriage, premature labour, cervical incompetence*
- *Vaginal bleeding, fluid loss*
- *Multiple pregnancies*
- *Abnormal placenta position*
- *Pain/decreased foetal movement/breech position*
- *Anaemia, blood disorders, hypertension*

01

PELVIC FLOOR EXERCISES

To tone your pelvic floor muscles. In the first 30 weeks of pregnancy do them lying down, but then switch to a sitting position.

(01) (facing page)
Lie on the floor with your knees raised and your arms by your sides. Support your head and shoulders with soft pillows. Imagine a string connecting your pelvic floor muscles to your breast bone. Breathe in. As you breathe out, imagine the string pulling the muscles upward. Hold. Breathe in. Relax. Repeat 10 times.

SITTING POSITION *(02–03)*
Have your feet flat on the floor or supported by a pile of books.

(02) This is the wrong way.

(03) Your back should be elongated and well supported. Let your arms relax, palms resting on your thighs. Breathe in, and as you breathe out, press your hands down, pulling up your pelvic floor. Elongate the spine and hold. Repeat 10 times.

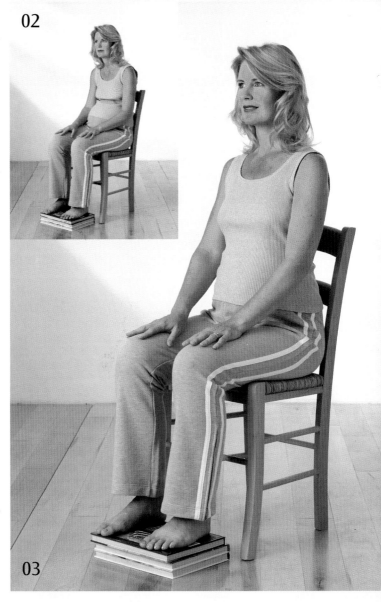

02

03

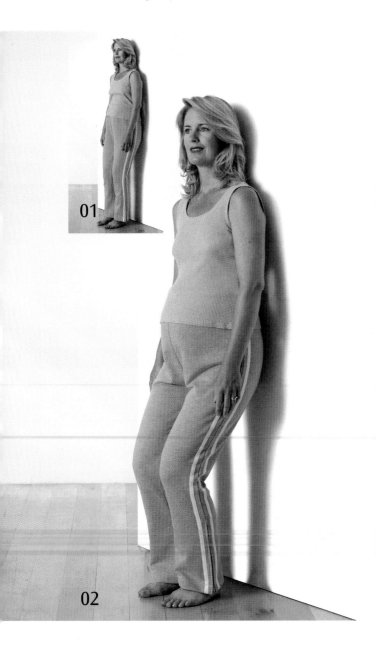

01

02

PILATES PREGNANCY ROUTINE *(01–17)*

PELVIC TILTS *(01–02)*
To stretch out the back and work the lower abs.

(01) Lean against a wall, with your back supported and knees soft, legs slightly apart. Elongate your spine.

(02) Breathe in, and as you breathe out, curl your pelvis gently away from the wall. Breathe in and relax your pelvis back against the wall. Repeat 10 times.

PLIÉS *(02–04)*
To strengthen the legs.

(02) Leaning against the wall, elongate your spine, and as you breathe in bend your knees, sliding down the wall. As you breathe out slide up the wall until your knees are straight but not locked. Repeat 10 times.

(03–04) This time place the legs further apart and slightly rotated. Do not do this exercise if you experience any pelvic pain.

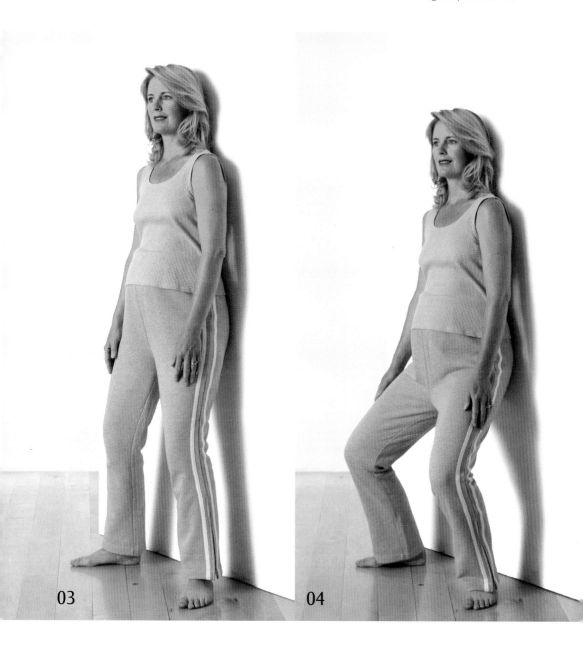

03

04

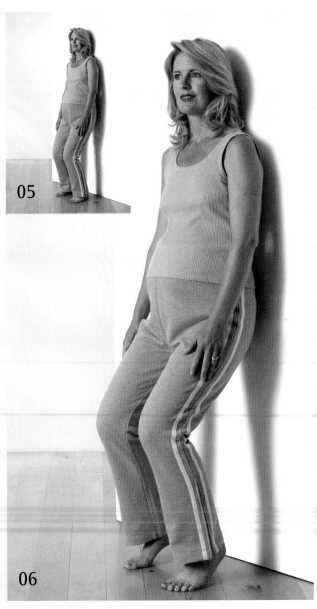

05

06

HEEL-RAISERS

(05) Stand with your back flat against the wall, knees bent, your weight on the centre of your feet.

(06) Breathe in, and lift your heels off the ground. Breathe out and lower again. Repeat 10 times.

ABDOMINALS

(07) Lie on your side with a pillow between your head and your arm and another between your knees. Allow your stomach muscles to relax. Breathe in, and as you breathe out, lift your stomach muscles away from the floor, toward your spine. Do this 10 times. Repeat for the other side.

OBLIQUES

(08) Place a cushion between your knees and rest your head on your arm.

(09) Breathe in, and as you breathe out, slide your right arm along the floor, lifting your upper body, supporting it on your hands. Breathe in and slide down again. Try 5 and then repeat for the other side.

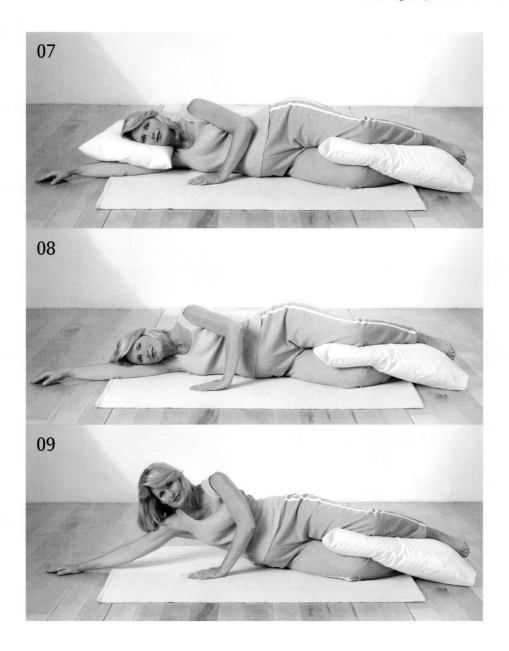

07

08

09

10

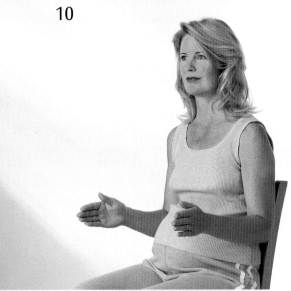

UPPER BODY RELEASE
(10–11)
To open the chest and strengthen the upper torso.

(10) With your upper arms held close, bend your elbows to a 90-degree angle.

(11) Breathe in, and as you breathe out, open your lower arms out to the side, keeping your upper arms close to your body. Breathe in to return to starting position. Repeat 10 times.

ONE-ARMED COSSACK
(12–13)
Practise pelvic floor exercises (see p.129) at the same time.

(12) Sit with your fingertips touching at chest height.

(13) Breathe in, and as you breathe out, rotate your upper body to the right. Pause. Breathe in, and as you breathe out, stretch one arm away, pushing it right back, rotating your body more. Breathe in, bend your right arm, and return to centre. Swap arms. Repeat the sequence 10 times.

11

12

13

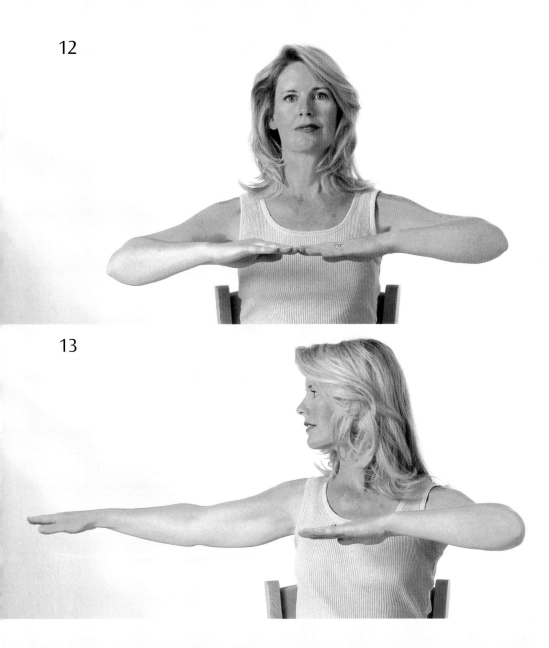

14

15

SCARF-BREATHING *(14–15)*
To help you focus your breathing, deepening the breath and improving lung capacity.

(14) Sitting, wrap a scarf around you, covering your ribs, crossed in front. Hold an end in each hand, pulling it taut. Breathe in slowly, feeling the lungs expanding and the scarf opening.

(15) As you breathe out, tighten the scarf, feeling air being squeezed out of your lungs. Repeat 10 times.

FEET & LEGS *(16–17)*
Not suitable after the 30th week of pregnancy.

(16) Lie with your head, shoulders, and right knee supported, left knee bent. With your right knee straight, flex and point your foot slowly and firmly, holding each position for a few seconds. Repeat 10 times.

(17) Point your foot, keeping your knee straight, rotate the ankle in both directions. Swap feet. Repeat 10 times for each foot.

Further reading

Alexander, Jane
The Weekend Healer
Gaia Books, 2000

Alexander, Jane
The Five Minute Healer
Gaia Books, 1999

Cohan, Robert
The Dance Workshop
Gaia Books, 1986

Gillanders, Ann
*A Gaia Busy Person's Guide,
Reflexology*
Gaia Books, 2002

Herdman, Alan
*Pilates, Creating the Body
You Want*
Gaia Books, 1999

Kirsta, Alix
The Book of Stress Survival
Gaia Books, 1987

Lavery, Sheila
The Healing Power of Sleep
Gaia Books, 1997

Reyneke, Dreas
*Ultimate Pilates, Achieve the
Perfect Body Shape*
Vermilion, 2002

Stanway, Penny
*Healing Foods for Common
Ailments*
Gaia Books, 1990

Index

Acknowledgments

Gaia Books would like to thank the following for their help in the production of this book:

Richard Burns for hair, makeup and styling on the photography shoots; Caron and Channing Bosler, Joshua Tuifua, Jane Paterson, and Sarah Gilham for modelling; the staff at Alan Herdman Studios; Sara Mathews for design; Susanna Abbott for editorial advice; Diana Walles for editorial help; and Lynn Bresler for proofreading and indexing.